MW01104249

Anything Can Happen

Fredy Perlman

Anything Can Happen published in October 1992 by Phoenix Press, PO Box 824, London, N1 9DL. Printed and bound by BPCC Wheatons, Exeter.

0 948984 22 8

Preface

Some of the essays in this book first appeared in Black & Red, a magazine in the late sixties and now a publisher . Others appeared in the still continuing quarterly newspaper *The Fifth Estate* which publishes in Detroit. Fredy also wrote over half a dozen full len gth books, including his spoof *Manual for Revolutionary Leaders*. Part of this book has now been published in a Phoenix Press edition under the title *The Seizure of State Power*, still under the supposed authorship of M. Velli. Full details of Fredy's writings and translations are included in *Having Little, Being Much*, a biography of Fredy written by his wife Lorraine.

Contents

Anything Can Happen

"Be Realists,

Demand the Impossible!"

This slogan, developed in May by revolutionaries in France, flies in the face of common sense, especially the "common sense" of American corporate-military propaganda. What *happened* in May also flies in the face of official American "common sense." In fact, in terms of American "common sense," much of what happens in the world every day is impossible. It can't happen. If it *does* happen, then the official "common sense" is nonsense: it is a set of myths and fantasies. But how can common sense be nonsense? That's impossible.

To demonstrate that *anything* is possible, this essay will place some of the myths alongside some of the events. The essay will then try to find out why some of the myths are possible, in other words, it will explore the "scientific basis" of the myths. The essay, if successful, will thus show that anything is possible: it's even possible for a population to take myths for common sense, and it's possible for mythmakers to convince themselves of the reality of their myths in the face of reality itself.

AMERICAN "COMMON SENSE"

* It's impossible for people to run their own lives; that's why they don't have the power to do so. People are powerless because they have neither the ability nor the desire to control and decide about the social and material conditions in which they live.

* People only want power and privileges over each other. It would be impossible, for example, for university students to fight against the institution which assures them a privileged position. Those students who study do so to get high grades, because with the high grades they can get high-paying jobs, which means the ability to manage and manipulate other people, and the ability to buy more consumer goods than other people. If learning were not rewarded with high grades, high pay, power over others and lots of goods, no one would learn; there'd be no motivation for learning.

* It would be just as impossible for workers to want to run their factories, to want to decide about their production. All that workers are interested in is wages: they just want more wages than others have, so as to buy bigger houses, more cars and longer trips.

* Even if students, workers, farmers wanted something different, they're obviously satisfied with what they're doing, otherwise they wouldn't be doing it.

* In any case, those who aren't satisfied can freely express their dissatisfaction by buying and by voting: they don't have to buy the things they don't like, and

7

they don't have to vote for the candidates they don't like. It's impossible for them to change their situation any other way.

* Even if some people tried to change the situation some other way, it would be impossible for them to get together; they'd only fight each other, because white workers are racists, black nationalists are anti-white, feminists are against all men, and students have their own specific problems.

* Even if they did unite, it would obviously be impossible for them to destroy the State and the police and military potential of a powerful industrial society like the United States.

THE EVENTS

Millions of students all over the world—in Tokyo, Turin, Belgrade, Berkeley, Berlin, Rome, Rio, Warsaw, New York, Paris—are fighting for the power to control and decide about the social and material conditions in which they live. They are not stopped either by the lack of desire, or by the lack of ability; they are stopped by cops. Perhaps they're inspired by other fighters who held on against cops: the Cubans, the Vietnamese,. .

Students in Turin and Paris, for example, occupied their universities and formed general assemblies in which all the students made all the decisions. In other words, the students started running their own universities. Not in order to get better grades: they did away with tests. Not in order to get higher paying jobs or more privileges: they started to discuss the abolition of privileges and high paying jobs; they started to discuss putting an end to the society in which they had to sell themselves. And at that point, sometimes for the first time in their lives, they started learning.

In Paris young workers, inspired by the example of the students, occupied an aircraft factory and locked up the director. The examples multiplied. Other workers began to occupy their factories. Despite the fact that all life long they had depended on someone to make their decisions for them, some workers set up committees to discuss running the strike on their own terms, letting all workers decide, and not just on the union's terms—and some workers set up commissions to discuss running the factories themselves. An idea which it's pointless to think about in normal times, because it's absurd, it's impossible, had suddenly become possible, and it became interesting, challenging, fascinating. Workers even began to talk about producing goods merely because people needed them. These workers knew that it was "false to think that the population is against free public services, that farmers are in favor of a commercial circuit stuffed with inter-mediaries, that poorly paid people are satisfied, that 'managers' are proud of their privileges. . ."* Some electronics workers freely distributed equipment to demonstrators protecting themselves from the police; some farmers delivered free food to striking workers; and some armaments workers talked about distributing weapons to all workers, so that the workers could protect themselves from the national army and police.

In spite of a lifetime of business propaganda about how "satisfied" workers are with the cars, houses and other objects they receive in exchange for their living energy, workers expressed their "satisfaction" through a general strike which paralyzed all French industry for over a month. After being trained for a lifetime to "respect law and order," workers broke all the laws by occupying factories which don't "belong" to them because, as they quickly learned, the cops are there to see to it that the factories continue to "belong" to capitalist owners. The workers learned that "law and order" is what keeps them from running their own productive activity, and that "law and order" is what they'd have to destroy in order to rule their own society. The cops came out as soon as workers acted on their dissatisfaction. Perhaps the workers had known all along about the cops in the background; perhaps that's why the workers had seemed so "satisfied." With a gun pointing at his back, almost any intelligent person would be "satisfied" to hold his hands up.

Workers in Paris and elsewhere began to accept the students' invitation to come to the University of Paris auditoriums (at the Sorbonne, Censier, Halle-aux-vins, Beaux Arts, etc.) to talk about abolishing money relations and turning the factories into social services run by those who make and those who use the products. Workers began to *express themselves*. That's when the owners and their administrators threatened civil war, and an enormous police and military machine was deployed to make the threat real. With this crass display of the "forces of law and order," the king stood momentarily naked: the repressive dictatorship of the capitalist class was visible to all. Whatever illusions people might have had about their own "consumer sovereignty" or "voting power," whatever fantasies they might have had about transforming capitalist society by buying or voting, they lost them. They knew that their "buying power" and "voting power" simply meant servility and acquiescence in the face of enormous violence. The student revolt and the general strike in France (like the Black Revolt in the U.S., like the anti-imperialist struggle on three continents) had merely forced the ever-present violence to expose itself: this made it possible for people to size up the enemy.

In the face of the violence of the capitalist state, students, French workers, foreign workers, peasants, the well paid and the poorly paid, learned whose interests they had served by policing each other, by fearing and hating each other. In the face of the naked violence of the common oppressor, the divisions among the oppressed disappeared: students ceased to fight for privileges over the workers and joined the workers; French workers ceased to fight for privileges over the foreign workers, and joined together with the foreign workers; farmers ceased to fight for a special dispensation, and joined the struggle of the workers and the students. Together they began to fight against a single world system that oppresses and divides students from workers, qualified workers from unqualified, French workers from Spanish, black workers from white, "native" workers from "home" workers, colonized peasants from the whole "metropolitan" population.

9

The struggle in France did not destroy the political and military power of capitalist society. But the struggle did not show that this was impossible:

—Students at a demonstration in Paris knew they could not defend themselves from a police charge, but some students didn't run from the police; they started building a barricade. This was what the March 22 Movement called an "exemplary action": a large number of students took courage, didn't run from the cops, and began building barricades.

—Students knew that they could not, by themselves, destroy the state and its repressive apparatus, yet they occupied and started running the universities, and in the streets they returned the cops' volley of teargas with a volley of cobblestones. This too was an exemplary action: workers in a number of factories took courage, occupied their factories, and were ready to defend them from their "owners."

—The first workers who occupied their factories in order to take them over and start running them knew that they could not destroy the power of the capitalist class unless all workers took over their factories and defended them by destroying the state and its repressive power, yet they occupied the factories. This too was an exemplary action, but these workers did not succeed in communicating the example to the rest of the workers: the government, the press, and the unions told the rest of the population that the occupying workers were merely having a traditional strike to get higher wages and better working conditions from the state and the factory owners.

Impossible? All this happened in a two-week period at the end of May. The *examples* were extremely contagious. Is anyone really sure that those who produce weapons, namely workers, or even that cops and soldiers, who are also workers, are immune?

"SCIENTIFIC BASIS" OF THE "COMMON SENSE"

A "social scientist" is someone who is paid to defend this society's myths. His defense mechanism, in its simplest formulation, runs approximately as follows: He begins by *assuming* that the society of his time and place is the *only possible* form of society; he then *concludes* that some other form of society is *impossible*. Unfortunately, the "social scientist" rarely admits his assumptions; he usually claims that he doesn't make any assumptions. And it can't be said that he's lying outright: he usually takes his assumptions so much *for granted* that he doesn't even know he's making them.

The "social scientist" takes for granted a society in which there's a highly developed "division of labor," which includes both a separation of tasks and a separation ("specialization") of people. The tasks include such socially useful things as producing food, clothing and houses, and also such socially useless things as brainwashing, manipulating and killing people. To begin with, the "scientist" defines *all* of these activities as useful, because *his* society could not

10

run without them. Next, he assumes that these tasks can only be performed if a given person is attached to a given task for life, in other words if the specialized tasks are performed by specialized people. He does not assume this about everything. For example, eating and sleeping are necessary activities; society would break down if these things were not performed. Yet even the "social scientist" does not think that a handful of people should do all the eating while the rest don't eat, or that a handful of people should do all the sleeping while the rest don't sleep at all. He assumes the need for specialization only about those activities which are specialized in his particular society. In the corporate-military society, a few people have all the political power, the rest have none; a handful of people decide what to produce, and the rest consume it; a handful of people decide what kinds of houses to build, and the rest live in them; a handful of people decide what to teach in classrooms, and the rest swallow it; a handful of people create and the rest are passive; a handful of people perform and the rest are spectators. In short, a handful of people have all the power over a specific activity, and the rest of the people have no power over it even when they are directly affected by it. And obviously the people who have no power over a specific activity do not know what to do with such power: they won't even start learning what to do with it until they have it. From this the "scientist" concludes that people have neither the ability nor the desire to have such power, namely to control and decide about the social and material conditions in which they live. More straightforwardly, the argument says: people do not have such power in *this society,* and this society is the *only* form of society; therefore it's impossible for people to have such power. In still simpler terms: People can't have such power because they don't have it.

Logic is not taught much in American schools, and the argument looks impressive when it is accompanied by an enormous statistical apparatus and extremely complicated geometrical designs. If a critic insists on calling the argument simplistic and circular, he's turned off as soon as the "scientist" pulls out figures calculated on computers inaccessible to the public, and he's turned out as soon as the "scientist" starts "communicating" in a completely esoteric language which has all the logical fallacies built-in, but which is comprehensible only to "scientific colleagues."

Mythological conclusions based on mythological assumptions are "proved" by means of the statistics and the charts; much of "applied social science" consists of teaching young people what kind of "data" to gather in order to make the conclusions come out, and much of "theory" consists of fitting this data to the pre-established formulas. By means of numerous techniques, for example, it can be " proved" that workers would rather have high paying jobs than enjoyable or meaningful jobs, that people "like" what they hear on the radio or see on television, that people are "members" of one or another Judeo-Christian cult, that almost anyone votes either for Democrats or for Republicans. Students are taught one set of methods for gathering the data, a second set for arranging them, a third set for presenting them, and "theories" for interpreting them. The apologetic

11

content of the "data" is covered up by its statistical sophistication. In a society where eating depends on getting paid, and thus where doing "meaningful work" may mean one doesn't get paid, a worker's preference for high paying over meaningful jobs merely means he'd rather eat than not eat. In a society where people do not create and control what they hear on the radio or see on television, they have no choice but to "like" what they hear and see, or else to turn the damn thing off. People who know their friends would look at them funny if they were atheists prefer to go to one or another Church, and almost anyone who knows he's in a society where he'd lose all his friends as well as his job if he were a socialist or an anarchist obviously prefers to be a Democrat or a Republican. Yet such "data" serves as the basis for the "social scientist's" conception of people's possibilities and impossibilities, and even of their "human nature."

The interviews, polls, and statistical demonstrations about people's religious affiliations, electoral behavior, job preferences, reduce people to monotonous data. In the context of this "science," people are *things*, they are objects with innumerable qualities—and surprisingly enough, each one of these qualities happens to be served by one or another institution of the corporate-military society. It just so happens that people's "material tastes" are "satisfied" by corporations, that their "physical urges" are "satisfied" by the military, that their "spiritual tendencies" are "satisfied" by the cults, and that their "political preferences" are "satisfied" either by the Republican or by the Democratic party. In other words everything about American corporate-militarism fits people just perfectly.

Everything is tabulated except the fact that a working person *serves as a tool*, that he sells his living time and creative ability in exchange for objects, that he doesn't decide what to make, nor for whom, nor why.

The "social scientist" claims to be empirical and objective; he claims to make no value judgments. Yet by reducing the person to the bundle of tastes, desires and preferences to which he's restricted in capitalist society, the "objective scientist" makes the bizarre claim that this bundle is what the worker is; and he makes the fantastic value judgment that the worker cannot be other than what he is in capitalist society. According to the "laws of human behavior" of this "science," the solidarity of students with workers, the occupation of factories by workers, the desire of workers to run their own production, distribution and coordination, are all impossible. Why? Because these things are impossible in capitalist society, and for these "scientists" who make no value judgments, existing societies are the only possible societies, and the corporate-military society is the best of all possible societies.

Given the value judgments of these experts ("who make no value judgments"), everyone in American society *must* be satisfied. For thes valueless "scientists," dissatisfaction is a "value judgment" imported from abroad, for how could anyone not be satisfied in the best of all possible worlds? A person must have "foreign based ideas" if he doesn't recognize this as the best of all possible worlds; he must be unbalanced if he's not satisfied with it; he must be dangerous if he means to act on his dissatisfaction; and he must be removed from his job, starved if possible, and killed if necessary, for the continued satisfaction of the expert.

To the American social scientist, "human nature" is what people do in corporate-military America: a few make decisions and the rest follow orders; some think and others do; some buy other people's labor and the rest sell their own labor; a few invest and the rest are consumers; some are sadists and others masochists; some have a desire to kill and others to die. The "scientist" passes all this off as "exchange," as "reciprocity," as a "division of labor" in which people are divided along with tasks. To the "social scientist" this is all so *natural* that he thinks he makes no value judgments when he takes it all for granted. Corporations and the military even give him grants to show that it's always been this way: grants to demonstrate that this "human nature" is lodged in the beginning of history and in the depths of the unconscious. (American psychologists—especially "behaviorists"—make the ambiguous "contribution" of demonstrating that animals also have a "human nature"—the psychologists drive rats mad in a situation similar to a war which the psychologists themselves helped plan, and then they show that rats, too, have a desire to kill, that they have masochist tendencies,. . .)

Given this conception of "human nature," the strength of the corporate-military system does not reside in the potential violence of its army and police, but in the fact that the corporate-military system is consistent with human nature.

In terms of what the American "social scientist" takes for granted, when students and workers in France started to fight to do away with "reciprocity," "exchange," and the division of labor, they were not fighting against the capitalist police, but against "human nature." And since this is obviously impossible, the events that took place in May, 1968, , did not take place.

"COMMON SENSE" EXPLODES

The question of *what is possible* cannot be answered in terms of *what is*. The fact that "human nature" is hierarchic in a hierarchic society does not mean that a hierarchic division of people among different tasks is necessary for social life.

It is not the capitalist institutions which satisfy human needs. It is the working people of capitalist society who shape themselves to fit the institutions of capitalist society.

When some people buy labour and others sell it, each fights to sell himself at the highest price, each fights to convince the buyer and himself that the next person is worth less.

In such a society, students who prepare to sell themselves as high-salaried managers and manipulators must tell their buyers and themselves that, as "professionals," they're superior to non-University manual workers.

In such a society, WASP (White Anglo-Saxon Protestant) workers who sell themselves for higher-paying, easier jobs, frantically tell themselves and their buyers that they're better, work harder, and are more deserving than foreigners, Catholics, Jews, Puerto Ricans, Mexicans and Blacks; black "professionals" tell themselves that they're better than black manual workers; all whites tell themselves they're better than all blacks; and all Americans tell themselves they're better than South American, Asian or African "natives." Since WASPS systematically succeed in selling themselves at the highest price, everyone below tries to make himself as much a WASP as possible. (WASPS happen to be the traditional ruling class. If midgets systematically got the highest price, everyone below would try to be a midget.)

To keep its relative privileges, each group tries to keep the groups below from shaking the structure.

Thus in times of "peace" the system is largely self-policed: the colonized repress the colonized, blacks repress blacks, whites repress each other, the blacks, and the colonized. Thus the working population represses itself, "law and order" is maintained, and the ruling class is saved from further outlays on the repressive apparatus.

To the "social scientist" and the professional propagandist, this "division of labor" is as *natural* as "human nature" itself. Unity among the different "interest groups" is as inconceivable to the "social scientist" as revolution.

While holding as "scientifically proved" that the different groups cannot unite in an anti-capitalist struggle, the expert does all he can to prevent such unity, and his colleagues design weapons just in case people did unite against the capitalist system.

Because sometimes the whole structure cracks.

The same expert who defines the capitalist system as consistent with "human nature," with people's tastes, wishes, desires, constructs the arsenal of myths and weapons with which the system defends itself. But what does the system defend itself *against*: human nature? If it has to fight against human nature to survive, then by the expert's own language, the system is extremely *unnatural*.

Thus while some experts define the rebellion in France as *impossible* because unnatural, their expert colleagues design the incapacitating gases with which cops can suppress such impossible rebellions. BECAUSE ANYTHING IS POSSIBLE.

1968

* Mouvement du 22 mars, *Ce n'est qu'un début, Continuons le combat,* Paris: Maspero, 1968.

Purpose of Black & Red

If you don't like it, make your own.

What is Black & Red?

Black & Red is not a capitalist activity. It is anti-capitalist in its organization and its aims.

Black & Red is a subversive action, and in this it is not Liberal.

Its present field of action is the student milieu, but Black & Red is not a new intellectual current, a new "cultural trend" within the Capitalist University.

Black & Red is a new front in the world anti-capitalist struggle.

It is an organic link between the theory-action of the world revolutionary movement and the action-theory of the new revolutionary front.

Its aim is: "To create at long last a situation which goes beyond the point of no return" (International Situationists).

Black & Red is an anti-capitalist activity

The production of Black & Red is not capitalist production.

It is not the production of a commodity, nor a social relation between capitalists-owners and workers-producers, and it is not done for profit. Black & Red has this in common with other media of the "underground press," but not with *Monthly Review* or *Ramparts*, for example. *Monthly Review*, Maspero in France, Feltrinelli in Italy, are capitalist activities. They're businesses which publish left-wing books. The underground presses are struggles. They don't create profits. Frequently they don't even reproduce the variable capital—the wages of the militants who produce them. As a result, these activities cannot sustain their producers. The time, the money, the energy of the militants who create these presses have to be LIBERATED out of capitalism in order to make the presses exist, in order to create these instruments of struggle.

Not all the social relations within the existing society are necessarily capitalist relations. There are PRE-capitalist relations, for example family relations, where there is no commodity production, labor is not alienated from worker to capitalist, and production is not for profit. There are also NON-capitalist relations, for example, "revolutionary" political parties, which may exist for 50 years within capitalist society; religious organization; or hippies. These relations COEXIST with capitalist relations. They are all a part of capitalist "culture"; they do not destroy the capitalist relations.

But the SOCIAL RELATIONS CREATED FOR THE PRODUC-
TION of Black & Red are not, in principle, integrable within capitalist
society. These relations DO NOT COEXIST with capitalist social
relations. "Underground presses" cannot survive within capitalist society; in fact, they do not even have continuity within capitalist society;
they have to re-created from one issue to the next, from one meeting to
the next; they are created only IN ORDER TO DESTROY capitalist
relations. When people spend working-days engaged in production, and
are not paid, either the activity stops, or capitalist society stops. They
either make a revolution, or they become transformed into capitalist
activities, like *Monthly Review*, which starts by paying wages, and then,
why not make a profit as well, so as to invest, in order to make the
operation grow? Some "underground presses" don't even pay for their
"constant capital," for the equipment and material they use up. They don't
create any of their conditions for reproduction: they don't reproduce
themselves. They are created by revolutionary energy—they represent a
struggle which is the same as the struggle of the movement itself:
revolutionary activity demands the working-time and leisure-time of
militants, WITHOUT PROVIDING THE MEANS OF LIFE which
capitalist working-activity provides.

This is why the "underground press" either DESTROYS capitalist
society, or it is destroyed. IT'S EITHER REVOLUTION OR DEATH.

Black & Red is subversive, not liberal

Violence is the expression, the manifestation of the existence of
irreconcilable contradictions in the capitalist system (class struggle, anti-
imperialist struggle, struggle against alienation, i.e., for life). It is the
expression of the consciousness of two antagonistic forces (Exploiter-
Exploited; Colonizer-Colonized; World Capitalist System-World Revolutionary Movement), i.e., force A and force non-A, one of which is
dominant, the other of which seeks to destroy the first.

The non-radical (we call him a Liberal) is situated in the dominant
force, A, and denies the existence of non-A.

He is an integral part of the dominant system; his motivation is
moral. His moral attitude is the product of the capitalist ideology of
PEACE, an ideology which completely contradicts IMPERIALIST
PRACTICE. Imperialist practice destroys all the forces which are radi-
cally opposed to it. The Liberal does not question working for the

capitalist system and its consequence: IMPERIALIST VIOLENCE. What bothers him are only the MORAL consequences of his work within the system.

This is why he wants VIOLENCE to end. But he can't stop EITHER the Americans OR the Vietnamese; he can't stop either the racists or the blacks. Since he's "liberal," since he agrees with the "aspirations" of the Vietnamese, of the blacks, he tells THEM to stop the violence. But as soon as THEY stop, the dominant system wins: America wins, Racism wins. The victim is not liberated: he's forced to negotiate with his oppressor.

The Liberal is an integral part of the dominant system. That is why his attitude aims to "change" (i.e., to interpret) the system from the inside, not to destroy (i.e., transform) it. When he presents himself as a radical, it is to create a new ideological current , a new group, sometimes even a group inspired by Marx's analysis.

Analysis, even "Marxist" analysis, without revolutionary practice, means CONVERSION to a new idea. Such analysis makes it possible for the Liberal to tell the revolutionary: Look at my accomplishments. I've created consciousness (i.e., "culture"). This is the way to change society. You activists want to go too fast. It's not yet time for action. If you want to act, if you want to fight right now, we will be clubbed and beaten. You are calling for repression. The consciousness (i.e., "culture") we have created will be destroyed.

The "consciousness" which the Liberal creates is consistent with PROFITS. All of his "revolutionary" activities have one thing in common: THEY ALL COEXIST WITH CAPITALISM. (We are not asking if the Capitalist System is better or worse with these things). Capitalism can survive with the type of "Critical Analysis" created by the Liberal.

The Liberal talks about "critical consciousness," but what he defends is the Capitalist University, Corporate-Military Research, Textbooks, Classrooms. These are the Liberal's VALUES. The revolutionary who says that these are the Liberal's instruments of oppression and repression, and that only a violent struggle against these instruments, these values, can destroy the system, is called an Extremist, a Dangerous Agitator. The Liberal calls him VIOLENT. And while calling him violent, THE LIBERAL CALLS THE POLICE.

The Liberal knows that the society is sick with contradictions which spread in it like tumors. The Liberal submits to this sickness. He knows that the tumors have to be removed. The following analogy by B.R. Rafferty* shows that ACTION is the cutting-edge that separates the

17

revolutionary from the Liberal. The first is the surgeon; the second runs in to prevent the operation.

"Don't operate! shouts the Liberal. What will you put in the place of the tumor?

The surgeon answers: Nothing!"

It's the same as the question: What kind of exploitation will replace capitalist exploitation: What kind of alienation will replace capitalist alienation?

The Liberal wants the surgeon to JUSTIFY the operation INSTEAD of carrying it out. The Liberal calls for an "alternative tumor," a restructured capitalist society. This gives the Liberal a basis for saying: at least we offer something positive, whereas all you do is offer something negative and destructive. The Liberal makes pictures of the "future society"—pictures of a restructured capitalism, or even pictures of a future "socialist" or "communist" society. And these pictures coexist with capitalist society; they are completely consistent with capitalist production relations. The revolutionary does not make pictures; he does not coexist with capitalist society; his aim is not to make pictures of society after the revolution, but to make revolutionary action. The Liberal has no conception of revolutionary action; for the Liberal, revolutionary action is destructive; it is just Violence.

For the revolutionary, the problem is not VIOLENCE versus NONVIOLENCE. Violence ALREADY EXISTS. Violence is the relation between the oppressor and the oppressed. Nonviolence does not eliminate the relation between oppressor and oppressed. Neutrality does not eliminate violence. For the oppressed there is no neutrality. In the struggle of the oppressed to liberate themselves, one who does not act against oppression is an oppressor.

The GI against whom the Vietnamese struggles is an oppressor, even if this GI is actually a worker who is exploited and oppressed, like the Vietnamese, by the capitalist system. It is up to the GI to decide. And GIs are in fact deciding. The growing number of deserters, the growing consciousness in the U.S., show that this is the problem which is being posed, by GIs, by black people, by students.

The only choice is to take part in the struggle to eliminate the relation of oppressor-oppressed, colonizer-colonized. The only choice is to struggle against the capitalist system and its manifestations: imperialism for the Vietnamese, racism for black people, brainwashing for students. THIS IS THE CHOICE OF THE REVOLUTIONARY. Black & Red makes this choice: this is what makes it subversive. Black & Red is part of the struggle of the Vietnamese, of black militants in the U.S., of French and other revolutionary students. The violence of the revolutionary is the violence of all the oppressed against the violence of the dominant class. The violence of the revolutionary does not aim to transform the oppressed into a new oppressor, nor to restore the economic and social relations of exploitation, but to build a society without classes, without alienation, and thus without violence.

Black & Red is a new revolutionary front

Black & Red is a new front in the world anti-capitalist struggle. Its geographical milieu is Kalamazoo: the high schools and universities. Its social milieu is students. Its activity is radical action against the University, against its stunting of creativity and its brainwashing. Its action is based on analysis which defines the University as an integral part of a larger whole: the world capitalist system.

Black & Red is an addition to the anti-capitalist struggle already being waged on other fronts:

Its action parallels that of black revolutionaries struggling in ghettos against racism—racism which is the direct outgrowth of a world system of exploitation.

Its action parallels that of Dodge revolutionary workers struggling against racism and against capitalist exploitation.

Its action parallels that of European revolutionary workers at Citroen, Renault, Fiat, against the union bureaucracy and the capitalist owners.

Its action parallels that of Bolivian revolutionaries and peasants struggling against landlords in the Andes—Bolivian revolutionaries who have expressed their understanding that they are not engaged in a local struggle, but in a struggle against the entire imperialist system.

"Create One, Two, Three, Many Vietnams"—this is how Che Guevara expressed the need to struggle on all the fronts.

The fact that the action of Black & Red is situated in a student milieu is not a self-restriction; it is the definition of a specific front which is part of a larger struggle.

The May revolutionary movement in France spread from the University to the factories. The University was transformed into a center of revolutionary coordination and diffusion for workers and students. This role had been played by worker-occupied factories in Russia in 1917.

American workers are not a social category who will be "reached," "organized," or "led" by the students. They are situated in what is, potentially, one of the main fronts of the world anti-capitalist struggle. Up to now, they have been had by capitalist ideology, and they've been used against the oppressed. Until now, American workers have been brainwashed and have collaborated with their exploiters; this has not prevented colonized Algerians and Vietnamese, racially oppressed blacks, brainwashed students, French workers, Czech and Yugoslav students and workers, from starting to struggle on their own fronts. Each new front pushes the world anti-capitalist struggle closer to the point of no return. When American workers begin their own struggle within their factories, they will join the revolutionaries who have already begun struggling on other fronts.

Thus Black & Red is not addressed particularly to students, but to all revolutionaries engaged in the same struggle, to all people who are attempting to build a critique of their situation and a revolutionary movement within the structure which oppresses them.

Black & Red is the means of expression, action and analysis of an active minority. It is the expression of the practice of a specific group on a specific front. PRACTICE which is not communicated is not practice but merely isolated action; COMMUNICATION which is not followed by an extension of practice to a larger group is merely analysis of an action.

Black & Red is an attempt TO COMMUNICATE PRACTICE. The communication of practice extends over time and over space. Past practice of the world revolutionary movement is the basis for present action on a given front; present practice on any single front is a further extension of the practice of the entire world movement.
Black & Red is in a world context because the capitalist system is a unified world system, a world market. All opposition to it is a part of the same struggle. Thus Black & Red is in solidarity with all other revolutionaries fighting on all fronts, and attempts to bring into the actions of Kalamazoo the analysis and experience of revolutionary students in Mexico, Berlin, Yugoslavia, Columbia, The analysis and experience of workers and students in France and Czechoslovakia.

At the same time, the experience in Kalamazoo which is based on critical analysis of the entire world movement, is communicated (i.e., extended) to other fronts. This experience includes a systematic critique of capitalist ideology carried out in classrooms (modeled on actions of the German SDS), self-critiques of militants engaged in actions, critiques of pseudo-revolutionary "actions." The purpose of the critiques and self-critiques is to push potential revolutionaries to self-analyses and re-evaluations of the relation of forces, and to stimulate among potential revolutionaries the ABILITY TO ANALYZE ACTIONS and to realise that NOT EVERY dangerous action or provocation is a REVOLUTION-ARY ACTION.

Thus Black & Red does not represent a new current of thought or a new method of analysis. It is not a new REVIEW, but the analytic and theoretical element of an action, addressed to people who are not interested in a cultural critique, but who have potential for acion, and for the extension of revolutionary practice to a new front.

In this spirit, a formal critique of the contents or method of Black & Red has no relevance unless it is an action-critique which bases its analysis on a specific action. To say that A NEW FRONT is ineffectual implies the capacity to CREATE ANOTHER FRONT. The interest of Black & Red is not to be THE front, but A front. The very content of its purpose and practice is TO BE SURPASSED. Its interest is precisely the CREATION OF OTHER FRONTS.

Black & Red is not an INSTITUTION which defends its own existence against the pressure of history and even against the very revolution it aims for. If a larger revolutionary front can be created in Kalamazoo, Black & Red will become part of it—either as Black & Red, or as a group of revolutionaries. If a larger revolutionary front is not created, then Black & Red intends to grow, to engage all revoluionary groups and individuals within actions and analyses. To participate in the actions of Black & Red means to modify these actions, to make them more effective, more critical, i.e., to enlarge the revolutionary front created by Black & Red.

Black & Red claims NO MONOPOLY OF ACTION OR ANALYSIS. It invites every critique which is a new front: "IF YOU DON'T LIKE IT, MAKE YOUR OWN!"

1968

    * One of the professors who, last year, was not rehired (i.e., was fired) by Western Michigan University.

I Accuse This Liberal University of Terror and Violence

On February 24th, 1969, a radical student was arrested at her home early in the morning and taken to the Kalamazoo Jail. She was charged with "assault and battery" for defending herself from the insistent harassment and insults of a student who opposed her POLITICS: he insulted her because she had dared to question a Political Science Professor and had tried to PROVOKE DISCUSSION among students in a university. The Political Science Professor did not answer the questions she raised; he responded with VIOLENCE: he had her summoned to a Dean and a Disciplinary Board to suspend her from school for "disrupting" his class, and he proudly announced that she would be arrested by the Police FOR VIOLENCE against his "good" student. For trying to question his course, the Political Science Professor is having her thrown out of school and tried for a crime; once he transforms her into an "outsider" and a "criminal," she will no longer be able to question his course: he can then have the "criminal outsider" arrested merely for being in the university.In 1968 two radical professors (B.R. Rafferty and I) were fired by the Economics Department and the School of General Studies of this Liberal University. The reasons were not written down; verbally we were accused of being "Unobjective, Dogmatic, Vulgar, Violent, Stalinist, Extremist..." If we had reacted to the stream of insults and defended ourselves, we would have been arrested by the City Police for "assault and battery." (I have recently been informed that I am to be arrested on the charge of "conspiracy" for fighting back IN WRITINGS.) Within this Liberal University "devoted to stimulating probing minds and critical intellects," radical politics is HERESY, heresy is VIOLENCE, and violence is repressed by the FORCES OF LAW AND ORDER.

These events did not take place in the Middle Ages, in Nazi Germany, or in Stalin's Russia. They are taking place NOW at THIS UNIVERSITY, where the majority of professors and students are LIBERAL. The repression of "heresy" is not being carried out by Reactionaries or "right wing extremists"; it is initiated and justified by people who consider themselves LIBERAL and "moderate."

B.R. Rafferty saw through the LIBERAL who is in favor of free speech, who is in favor or All Points of View being Represented in the University, who is Willing to Talk to Radicals, who "understands" Marx, C. Wright Mills, Frantz Fanon, Che Guevara, and is "sympathetic " to them. It's precisely BECAUSE HE EXPOSED THE LIBERAL that Rafferty had to be destroyed.

The Liberal says he has more "sympathy" for the Extreme Left than for the Extreme Right. However, as soon as a radical is hired into HIS department, the Intellectual Liberal no longer has "sympathy." The radical in HIS department is not a "scholar" but a "Vulgar Marxist," he's not an "intellectual" but a "propagandist"; he's not "objective" but "Dogmatic"; he's not a "Theorist" but a "Nineteenth Century Marxist."

Rafferty's insight about these terms is that THEY ARE EXTREMIST TERMS COUCHED IN A "MODERATE" LANGUAGE: that "Vulgar Marxist" means: "Throw him out!" When the Liberal Intellectual mildly calls someone a Vulgar Marxist, or a Dogmatic Leftist Propagandist, he's not simply stating his "moderate disagreement" with someone, the way he does when he says "He's a convinced Keynesian" or "He's a stubborn Aristotelian"; he's making an extremist and fanatical statement which means: HE'S A VULGAR MARXIST AND DOESN'T BELONG IN THIS DEPARTMENT! HE'S NOT OBJEC-TIVE AND SHOULDN'T TEACH IN ANY UNIVERSITY: HE'S A DOGMATIC LEFTIST AND MUST BE STOPPED FROM EARNING AN INCOME; HE MUST BE KILLED!

"Vulgar" means DIRTY and COMMON; the "Vulgar Marxist" or "Vulgar Leftist Propagandist" is someone whose ideas are not based on "Pure Research" but on DIRTY REALITY; someone who does not write for the Sophisticated Audience of Scholarly Journals (for Pure Academics and for the top bureaucrats of Corporations and the State who pay for these journals); the "Vulgar Leftist" writes for the DIRTY PEOPLE IN THE STREET.

"Vulgar Marxist," and "Unobjective" and "he doesn't consider both sides," mean: IT IS LEGITIMATE TO THROW HIM OUT! These statements are IDEOLOGICAL WEAPONS WHICH JUSTIFY THE EXCLUSION OF A RADICAL FROM A UNIVERSITY.

Reactionaries did not fire Rafferty or myself from the Economics De-partment of Western Michigan University; LIBERALS FIRED US (in Liberal jargon, they didn't "fire" us; they merely didn't "rehire" us). AND IT IS NOT REACTIONARIES WHO ARE HARASSING STUDENTS TODAY. Liberal Professors initiated the slogan campaign and rushed us out before we had the time or the psychological composure to reply; Liberal Professors justified our elimination, a year before we were fired, with the "moderate" accusations of Unobjective, Dogmatic, Vulgar.

* * *

The Reactionary, who openly identifies with the project of Big Business, straightforwardly recognises the radical as a threat to his project. He is overt and honest when he says "Those radicals want to destroy Civilization" (by which he means his corporate-capitalist society), "and THEREFORE they must be de-stroyed." And he means DESTROYED—through violence: the police must get them, and they must be locked up or shot or both. The Reactionary knows that when He excludes a radical from the university, all his "Fellow Reactionaries" are pledged to do the same.

Unlike the Reactionary, the Liberal does not call for terror and violence overtly but covertly; he does not call for violence all at once but in stages. He does not say "Exclude him from the University" but "Don't renew his contract." Unlike the Reactionary the Liberal maintains a good conscience by telling himself he has no intention to exclude the radical from all universities: he merely doesn't want the radical back in "his" department.

The Liberal does not admit, even to himself, that he is a member of a group; he does not like to be called a Liberal; he does not admit, even to himself, that Liberals run other departments and other universities, that Liberals run the dominant hierarchies of American society; he does not admit that HIS POWER COMES FROM THE FACT THAT OTHER LIBERALS WILL BACK HIM UP. Unlike the Reactionary, he does not admit that when he fires a radical he expects other Liberals to do the same. The Liberal's "liberalism" is an ideology which informs him that he's an "individual" who exists in a vacuum, and that his decision does not bind anyone else. He denies that all Liberals are bound to one Liberal's decision. He lies to himself: if it ever happened that a group of Liberals rehired the radical and fired the Liberal, the Liberal would shout "We all agree that..." and "Our basic principle is..." and "How can we tolerate such a blatant denial of our most sacred..."—in other words, "WE'RE ALL PLEDGED TO ACT TOGETHER"; "WE'RE MEMBERS OF THE SAME GROUP" ; "WE 'RE ALL ENGAGED IN THE SAME PROJECT"— and the project is the continued functioning of the corporate-military system. Consequently, if one Liberal spots a radical, he spots him for all Liberals; he spares them the trouble of spotting him. The Liberal's LIE is to tell himself that THE OTHERS are not bound to exclude the radical "just because " he excludes him. By his philosophy, the Others, like himself, are Pure Individuals Who May Hire Him Even If I Fire Him.

* * *

The Reactionary does not claim to be "neutral": he's overtly pro-Capitalist; he's an ardent supporter of every American corporate and military bureaucracy; he's openly fighting to maintain the power of the groups who are presently dominant, and he overtly wants to eliminate any real threats to that power.

The Liberal claims to be "neutral" and "objective"; he claims that he's NEITHER on the side of the "establishment" nor on the "other side"; he claims that he's not on any side: he's not in society but above it.

However, to the Liberal, only the action of the corporate-military bureaucracy is "legitimate"; the action of the radical is not. And just like the Reactionary, the Liberal thinks of the action of radicals AS A THREAT, which means that the Liberal sees himself ON THE DOMINANT SIDE, the side that's threatened. He does not recognize the provocations of the bureaucracy as provocations; only the actions of radicals are provocations. The Liberal accepts the rules of the dominant bureaucracy, and he defends those rules. He's not "objective." A challenge of the dominant rules is, for him, a "provocation."

The Liberal moves WITHIN THE DOMINANT BUREAUCRACY; his success comes from PLEASING THE PEOPLE WHO ARE ON TOP. The Liberal (whether professor or student) climbs WITHIN THE HIERARCHY and he wants to do so WITH A GOOD CONSCIENCE. The so-called "radical sympathies" of the Liberal are his means to maintain a good conscience while selling himself to those in power. The Liberal's greatest fear, in fact, is to become "an outsider"; he wants to be an "insider" who is Good and Moral, Just and Objective.

The Liberal rejects Imperialism, Patriotism, Racism, and even Capitalism—IN WORDS, but never in actions; and he knows the line between words and actions. Words make it possible for him to be a GOOD PERSON; action would make him an OUTSIDER. That's why the radical is a threat to the Liberal; HE FORCES THE LIBERAL TO CHOOSE. In the face of a radical, the Liberal is forced to choose between acting on his "principles" (and therefore becoming an "outsider"), or accepting the dominant bureaucracy. The mere presence of the radical exposes the "neutrality" of the Liberal: HE CHOOSES TO ACCEPT THE DOMINANT BUREAUCRACY.

The Liberal does not see himself as a dehumanized factor in a bureaucratic structure: his existence as a human being and his position in the hierarchy are the same to him. THAT'S WHY he cannot identify with the radical. For the radical, the provocations of the bureaucracy reach a LIMIT beyond which they're no longer acceptable: they negate his existence as a human being and he fights to remain alive. But since the Liberal IS a slot in the hierarchy (since he IS an "associate professor," a "director," etc.), since he accepts himself as a slot and title in the bureaucracy, he cannot be provoked by the bureaucracy; his humanity cannot be negated by the bureaucracy BECAUSE HE NEGATES IT HIMSELF. For him there's also a limit; this limit is reached when an "outsider" threatens the bureaucracy.

* * *

For the Liberal, the LIMIT is reached when a written or unwritten "rule" of the bureaucracy is broken, a LIMIT which is crossed by any radical as soon as he acts. This Limit is, in fact, completely arbitrary: the fact of "crossing the limit" is what enables the Liberal to justify repression: "You can argue, but you have to present both sides," "You can give out leaflets in the hall, but not in the classroom." The Limit, the Line, is not an action of the bureaucracy which goes beyond the limit of human decency; the Line is an action of a radical which challenges the peaceful and orderly functioning of the dominant system. And when the Liberal draws this line, wherever he draws it, HE JUSTIFIES THE ELIMINATION OF THE ONE WHO CROSSED THE LINE. This Limit is a justification of VIOLENCE .

When the Liberal says: "It's all right to give out leaflets in the halls but not in the classrooms"; when he finds a form, a rule, or a fictional rule that has been broken, he justifies repressing the lawbreaker. What his formula means is "Sick-'im!" It's like the so-called Southern Moderate, who explains lynchings to himself but is against them in principle. In every individual instance there's some FORMAL reason to justify the lynching: "Well, in this particular case he did such and such and went too far..." He always has reasons to accept every CONCRETE lynching that takes place, while PHILOSOPHICALLY he remains opposed to lynching, which he says is "horrible and a crime." The Liberal

Professor is against harassment and persecution of students; he has all kinds of Civil Libertarian principles about it. He's against suppressing anyone's freedom of speech. But the same Liberal is among the first to support the expulsion of a radical student; he was among the first the support the firing of Rafferty and myself (and many others). His PRINCIPLES are beautiful: they can all be framed. One can know who the Reactionary is from what he says; but what the Liberal says gives no clue to who he is.

* * *

The Liberal Professor spends his life manipulating students to fit the requirements of a corporate or state bureaucracy; his relations with people are manipulative relations. He programs students. The program he injects into them is "Science" (i.e. TRUTH). He injects this program into students by means of MANIPULATION. He assumes that manipulative relations are the only possible human relations: he stimulates and punishes students with tests and grades; he blackmails male students with the threat of induction into the military, and when these methods fail, he calls on the police.

The Liberal "tolerates" other "opinions." However, "opinions" are something less than TRUTH, and the "toleration of such opinions HAS A LIMIT. An individual professor may legitimately be "heterodox"; he may legitimately hold "heretical views"; BUT HE MUST NOT COMMUNICATE THESE VIEWS TO STUDENTS. Since, for the Liberal, communication can only take place by means of manipulation, the communication of "heresy" MUST take place by means of manipulation. However, when "tolerated opinions" are communicated to students, the students are not educated (since only TRUTH can edify); they are MISLED. Consequently, if students resist their own dehumanization, it is only because they were MISLED by "outside agitators" and "Vulgar Marxists." The Liberal does not give students credit for being able to draw their own conclusion about what he does to them. Furthermore, if the Liberal cannot see the INSTRUMENTS with which "heresies" are communicated, if he cannot see the tests, the grades, the blackmail and the intimidation, he does not conclude that the communication is not manipulative (something unknown to him); he concludes that THE INSTRUMENTS FOR SUCH MANIPULATION MUST BE DEMONIC. Consequently one who rejects the official doctrine, one who rejects the Church's TRUTH, is a Satanic MISLEADER of innocent souls, a Pied Piper who entices innocent spirits straight to Hell. One who uses DEMONIC instruments of manipulation is a WITCH. And a WITCH, in the 20th century as in earlier centuries, MUST BE DESTROYED.

* * *

As soon as the Liberal justifies the use of violence against a radical, he calls the radical VIOLENT. Another of Rafferty's insights is that the Liberal's accusations of "violence" are PURE PROJECTIONS OF HIS OWN VIOLENCE. It is precisely when he's in the act of excluding the radical by means of violence that the Liberal shouts "VIOLENCE!"

The radical is excluded quickly, in the dark, under the cover of bureaucratic pretexts, before he's able to react. The Liberal knows about the inertia that characterizes daily life; he knows that a counter-attack against systematic exclusion cannot be quickly organized. He counts on the radical's physical or psychological inability to launch a counter-attack.

However, the Liberal is IN FACT (if not by choice) a human being, and cannot keep himself from knowing that what he has done to another human being is humanly unacceptable and degrading. He knows that one way the radical can reaffirm his degraded humanity is by taking revenge. (As Frantz Fanon pointed out in *The Wretched of the Earth,* the Colonizer fears, and prepares for, the violence of the Colonized BEFORE THE COLONIZED EVEN BEGINS TO ACT, precisely because he knows WHAT HE WOULD DO IF HE WERE IN THE PLACE OF THE COLONIZED.) That's why he yells VIOLENCE and fears it. The Liberal has dehumanized himself IN ORDER to dehumanize the other, but he nevertheless knows how he would react as a human being: whether the slave returns with a gun or not, THAT'S WHAT HE SHOULD DO. THAT'S WHY the Liberal yells VIOLENCE at someone who has never held a weapon in his hand. (The Liberals of the WMU Economics Department yelled VIOLENCE at people who had not yet taken a stick against anyone.) The accusation of violence is not an analysis of what the radical DOES; it is an analysis of what the radical SHOULD DO if he were able to react in a human way.

The Liberal knows that HE is unable to react as a complete human being; he knows that HE dehumanizes himself in order to advance; he knows that HE cannot struggle against the bureaucracy to affirm his own life and his own project. And the Liberal projects his inability on the radical, AND COUNTS ON IT. For his own Peace and Quiet, he has to count on the physical repression OR the psychological breakdown of the radical.

* * *

The breakdown of the radical is, in fact, the usual consequence of repression. When this happens, the Liberal is INDIFFERENT, since he is innocent, and he's RELIEVED, since the radical no longer poses a threat.

What does the student do once thrown out of the university? Become a waitress or a bank clerk? Move into a "hippie commune?" Or break down psychologically? That's not the Liberal's "business." A sophomore who is totally sickened by the university frequently seeks "advice" from a Liberal. And the Liberal blandly "advises" the student that some things can be done, BUT THE STUDENT CANNOT GO BEYOND A CERTAN LINE. If he does, he will be thrown out of the university. If the student tries to fight beyond this line, the obstacles are so huge that the student may break down. And it is precisely the psychological breakdown of this student that the Liberal counts on. If he didn't, he'd never throw anyone out. If he didn't think these students would be psychologically destroyed and incapacitated even before the police got to them, he'd be deathly afraid to throw anyone out; he'd know all these people would be back in "hordes" to push the Liberals out. He counts on the physical or psychological death of these students. But he is never RESPONSIBLE for anything that happens to a student who once sought his advice. If a brilliant student, who could have learned a great deal even in the capitalist university, becomes a waitress for life, the Liberal is GUILTLESS: nothing he ever did led her to do that, and "not everyone can be a student in any case."

He knows that some radicals will, however awkwardly, try to fight back. And he also knows, from daily TV programs, what happens to radicals who fight back. He knows that, at some point, the radical will do the kind of thing which the Liberal calls VIOLENCE, and at that point will either be killed or jailed, or ostracised from society. For the Liberal, the repression of the radical means that violence has been averted, because for the Liberal there's only one kind of violence; the threats, the intimidations, the harassments , the arrests, the trials, the jailings ARE NOT VIOLENCE for the Liberal. Only the radical's struggle to maintain his humanity is VIOLENCE for the Liberal; the radical's struggle to regain the humanity which the Liberal deprived him of is VIOLENCE. That's why, when he cries VIOLENCE, he's scared: "My job! My house! My books!"

Once the radical is thrown out, he's no longer in the Liberal's jurisdiction: he's an "outside agitator," and a "criminal." The Outsider no longer "belongs" in the Liberal's university. Members of the Columbia SDS Chapter, for example, are now "outside agitators"; they are "not students" and consequently "have no right to be on campus." YET LAST YEAR THEY WERE STUDENTS OF COLUMBIA UNIVERSITY; they were thrown out by Liberals, and if they return to fight back, they're arrested by cops.

Consequently, anyone who objects and who fights back is by definition an "outsider," since his objections provide reasons to throw him out, and once he's out, he has no "right" to fight back.

The Liberal is always INNOCENT; he has nothing to do with anything; he never acts.

"God forbid! I didn't send for the Police! I didn't intend any VIOLENCE! I just didn't want an Unobjective Person in My Department. If he was jailed or shot by the Police, THAT'S NOT MY CONCERN; I'M COMPLETELY INNOCENT! I DIDN'T HAVE ANYTHING TO DO WITH THAT, and in any case, that merely shows what kind of person HE really was."

The Liberal's project is to exclude the radical from society, but he does not take responsibility for the project; he realizes his project in stages, but he is only responsible for the "innocent" first stage. OTHERS DO THE REST. The Liberal merely initiates the process, and is not responsible for what the others do.

The Reactionary hits the radical directly; the Liberal does not do his own hitting. The Liberal merely PROVOKES the radical until he responds to the provocation, and when he responds, THE COPS GET THE RADICAL. The Liberal maintains his good conscience: HE didn't act—the radical acted; HE didn't repress the radical—the cops did. THE LIBERAL IS ALWAYS INNO-

CENT: his only desire is peace and quiet.

The Reactionary throws out a radical and then has him arrested for Loitering or Conspiracy or outside Agitation if the radical returns to fight; the Reactionary "eggs on" and harasses until the radical is provoked to hit back, and then has him arrested for Assault and Battery; the Reactionary tries to exclude the radical from any sources of income in order to have him locked up as a thief. To the Reactionary, the radical is ALREADY A CRIMINAL WHEN HE EXPRESSES HIS THOUGHTS

The Liberal knows just as well as the Reactionary that "The cops'll get 'im"; HE COUNTS ON THE COPS TO PROTECT HIS PEACE AND QUIET; but, as Rafferty repeatedly observed, THE LIBERAL DOESN'T WANT TO SEE THE COPS WHO PROTECT HIM.

The Liberal can be compared to the Medieval Church. The Church excommunicated a heretic, but did not itself put the heretic to death . The Civil Authority, the Secular Authority, took charge of the heretic's body. The Church was innocent; the Civil Authorities and the Executioner were the ones responsible for physical extermination. The excommunicators of the Church maintained clean consciences.

Thus also the Liberal: All he does is to excommunicate the radical, to exclude him "spiritually"; the Civil Authorities do the rest. At every single step he applies systematic terror and violence, and at every single step he manages to maintain his clean conscience.

The Liberal ALREADY KNOWS that when his "Leftist Colleague" is an unemployed radical he will do something for which it will be legitimate to throw him in jail, but the Liberal doesn't want to be aware that HIS PEACE AND QUIET ARE MAINTAINED THROUGH TERRORISM AND VIOLENCE. In other words, the Liberal's weapons are the same as the reactionary's; the only difference between them is that the Liberal doesn't look, and has a good conscience. He's "tolerant," he "reads radical literature," he's the "only one who talks to radicals ," he's MORAL in every single way; he goes out of his way to "help radicals"; he'll do everything for radicals which will help him keep his good conscience WHILE HE CONTINUES TO RELY ON TERROR AND VIOLENCE.

Liberal professors and students whose situations can only be maintained through terror and violence, through systematic psychological and physical murder, advertise "Make Love Not War." Liberal students who have ALREADY CHOSEN to help maintain the dominant project when their time comes, are busy "accumulating" large "stocks" of good conscience while they can, while their "new styles of life" do not yet conflict with their future "responsibilities."

Liberals are not "moderate." That's their own self-image. They're extremists, but unlike reactionaries, THEY'RE EXTREMISTS WITH GOOD CONSCIENCES. Their instruments are not "ideas"; their instruments are TERROR and VIOLENCE. But unlike lynchers, THE LIBERALS TURN

THEIR EYES AWAY to maintain their innocence.

People are EXCLUDED; thousands of people are OUTSIDERS; yet the Liberals who forced them out are TOTALLY GUILTLESS, and have the illusion that they are the ones who are "sympathetic" to the Radical Students, the Emotionally What-Have-You Students, the Hippie Students. The Liberal who is the first to move WHENEVER SOMEONE CROSSES ONE OF HIS LINES at the same time "contributes generously" to "Left-wing organizations" and "is against the war in Vietnam." He is a supporter of all GOOD THINGS; he is a GOOD PERSON; he's the BEST PERSON IN THE WORLD. He is able to accept physical and psychological TERROR and VIOLENCE WITH A GOOD CONSCIENCE AND CHRISTIAN MORALS.

1969

The Reproduction of Daily Life

The everyday practical activity of tribesmen reproduces, or perpetuates, a tribe. This reproduction is not merely physical, but social as well. Through their daily activities the tribesmen do not merely reproduce a group of human beings; they reproduce a tribe, namely a particular *social form* within which this group of human beings performs *specific* activities in a *specific* manner. The specific activities of the tribesmen are not the outcome of "natural" characteristics of the men who perform them, the way the production of honey is an outcome of the "nature" of a bee. The daily life enacted and perpetuated by the tribesman is a specific *social* response to particular material and historical conditions.

The everyday activity of slaves reproduces slavery. Through their daily activities, slaves do not merely reproduce themselves and their masters physically; they also reproduce the instruments with which the master represses them, and their own habits of submission to the master's authority. To men who live in a slave society, the master-slave relation seems like a natural and eternal relation. However, men are not born masters or slaves. Slavery is a specific social form, and men submit to it only in very particular material and historical conditions.

The practical everyday activity of wage-workers reproduces wage labor and capital. Through their daily activities, "modern" men, like tribesmen and slaves, reproduce the inhabitants, the social relations and the ideas of their society; they reproduce the *social form* of daily life. Like the tribe and the slave system, the capitalist system is neither the natural nor the final form of human society; like the earlier social forms, capitalism is a specific response to material and historical conditions.

Unlike earlier forms of social activity, everyday life in capitalist society *systematically* transforms the material conditions to which capitalism originally responded. Some of the material limits to human activity come gradually under human control. At a high level of industrialization, practical activity creates its own material conditions as well as its social form. Thus the subject of analysis is not only how practical activity in capitalist society reproduces capitalist society, but also how this activity itself eliminates the material conditions to which capitalism is a response.

Daily Life in Capitalist Society

The social form of people's regular activities under capitalism is a response to a certain material and historical situation. The material and historical conditions explain the origin of the capitalist form, but do not explain why this form continues after the initial situation disappears. A concept of "cultural lag" is not an explanation of the continuity of a social form after the disappearance of the initial conditions to which it responded. This concept is merely a name for the continuity of the social form. When the concept of "cultural lag" parades as a name for a "social force" which determines human activity, it is an obfuscation which presents the outcome of people's activities as an external force beyond their control. This is not only true of a concept like "cultural lag." Many of the terms used by Marx to describe people's activities have been raised to the status of external and even "natural" forces which determine people's activity; thus concepts like "class struggle," "production relations" and particularly "The Dialectic," play the same role in the theories of some "Marxists" that "Original Sin," "Fate" and "The Hand of Destiny" played in the theories of medieval mystifiers.

In the performance of their daily activities, the members of capitalist society simultaneously carry out two processes: they reproduce the form of their activities, and they eliminate the material conditions to which this form of activity initially responded. But they do not know they carry out these processes; their own activities are not transparent to them. They are under the illusion that their activities are responses to natural conditions beyond their control, and do not see that they are themselves authors of those conditions. The task of capitalist ideology is to maintain the veil which keeps people from seeing that their own activities reproduce the form of their daily life; the task of critical theory is to unveil the activities of daily life, to render them transparent, to make the reproduction of the social form of capitalist activity visible within people's daily activities.

Under capitalism, daily life consists of related activities which reproduce and expand the capitalist form of social activity. The sale of labor-time for a price (a wage), the embodiment of labor-time in commodities (salable goods, both tangible and intangible), the consumption of tangible and intangible commodities (such as consumer goods and spectacles)—these activities which characterize daily life under capitalism are not manifestations of "human nature," nor are they imposed on men by forces beyond their control.

If it is held that man is "by nature" an uninventive tribesman and an inventive businessman, a submissive slave and a proud craftsman, an independent hunter and a dependent wage-worker, then either man's "nature" is an empty concept, or man's "nature" depends on material and historical conditions, and is in fact a response to those conditions.

Alienation of Living Activity

In capitalist society, creative activity takes the form of commodity production, namely production of marketable goods, and the results of human activity take the form of commodities. Marketability or salability is the universal characteristic of all practical activity and all products.

The products of human activity which are necessary for survival have the form of salable goods: they are only available in exchange for money. And money is only available in exchange for commodities. If a large number of men accept the legitimacy of these conventions, if they accept the convention that commodities are a prerequisite for money, and that money is a prerequisite for survival, then they find themselves locked into a vicious circle. Since they have no commodities, their only exit from this circle is to regard themselves, or parts of themselves, as commodities. And this is, in fact, the peculiar "solution" which men impose on themselves in the face of specific material and historical conditions. They do not exchange their bodies or parts of their bodies for money. They exchange the creative content of their lives, their practical daily activity, for money.

As soon as men accept money as an equivalent for life, the sale of living activity becomes a condition for their physical and social survival. Life is exchanged for survival. Creation and production come to mean sold activity. A man's activity is "productive," useful to society, only when it is sold activity. And the man himself is a productive member of society only if the activities of his daily life are sold activities. As soon as people accept the terms of this exchange, daily activity takes the form of universal prostitution.

The sold creative power, or sold daily activity, takes the form of *labor*. Labor is a historically specific form of human activity. Labor is abstract activity which has only one property: it is marketable, it can be sold for a given quantity of money. Labor is *indifferent* activity: indifferent to the particular task performed and indifferent to the particular subject to which the task is directed. Digging, printing and carv-

33

ing are different activities, but all three are *labor* in capitalist society. Labor is simply "earning money." Living activity which takes the form of labor is a means to earn money. Life becomes a *means of survival*.

This ironic reversal is not the dramatic climax of an imaginative novel; it is a fact of daily life in capitalist society. Survival, namely self-preservation and reproduction, is not the means to creative practical activity, but precisely the other way around. Creative activity in the form of *labor,* namely *sold activity,* is a *painful necessity* for survival; labor is the means to self-preservation and reproduction.

The sale of living activity brings about another reversal. Through sale, the labor of an individual becomes the "property" of another, it is appropriated by another, it comes under the control of another. In other words, a person's activity becomes the activity of another, the activity of its owner; it becomes *alien* to the person who performs it. Thus one's *life,* the accomplishments of an individual in the world, the difference which his life makes in the life of humanity, are not only transformed into *labor,* a painful condition for survival; they are transformed into *alien* activity, activity performed by the buyer of that labor. In capitalist society, the architects, the engineers, the laborers, are not builders; the man who buys their labor is the builder; their projects, calculations and motions are alien to them; their living activity, their accomplishments, are his.

Academic sociologists, who take the sale of labor for granted, understand this alienation of labor as a feeling: the worker's activity "appears" alien to the worker, it "seems" to be controlled by another. However, any worker can explain to the academic sociologists that the alienation is neither a feeling nor an idea in the worker's head, but a real fact about the worker's daily life. The sold activity is *in fact* alien to the worker; his labor is *in fact* controlled by its buyer.

In exchange for his sold activity, the worker gets money, the conventionally accepted means of survival in capitalist society. With this money he can buy commodities, things, but he cannot buy back his activity. This reveals a peculiar "gap" in money as the "universal equivalent." A person can sell commodities for money, and he can buy the same commodities with money. He can sell his living activity for money, but he cannot buy his living activity for money.

The things the worker buys with his wages are first of all consumer goods which enable him to survive, to reproduce his labor-power so as to be able to continue selling it; and they are spectacles, objects for passive admiration. He consumes and admires the products of human activity passively. He does not exist in the world as an active agent who transforms it, but as a helpless, impotent spectator; he may call this state of powerless admiration "happiness," and since labor is

34

painful, he may desire to be "happy," namely inactive, all his life (a condition similar to being born dead). The commodities, the spectacles, *consume him;* he uses up living energy in passive admiration; he is consumed by things. In this sense, the more he has, the less he is. (An individual can surmount this death-in-life through marginal creative activity; but the population cannot, except by abolishing the capitalist form of practical activity, by abolishing wage-labor and thus dealienating creative activity.)

The Fetishism of Commodities

By alienating their activity and embodying it in commodities, in material receptacles of human labor, people reproduce themselves and create Capital.

From the standpoint of capitalist ideology, and particularly of academic Economics, this statement is untrue: commodities are "not the product of labor alone"; they are produced by the primordial "factors of production," Land, Labor and Capital, the capitalist Holy Trinity, and the main "factor" is obviously the hero of the piece, Capital.

The purpose of this superficial Trinity is not analysis, since analysis is not what these Experts are paid for. They are paid to obfuscate, to mask the social form of practical activity under capitalism, to veil the fact that producers reproduce themselves, their exploiters, as well as the instruments with which they're exploited. The Trinity formula does not succeed in convincing. It is obvious that *land* is no more of a commodity producer than water, air, or the sun. Furthermore *Capital,* which is at once a name for a social relation between workers and capitalists, for the instruments of production owned by a capitalist, and for the money-equivalent of his instruments and "intangibles," does not produce anything more than the ejaculations shaped into publishable form by the academic Economists. Even the instruments of production which are the capital of one capitalist are primordial "factors of production" only if one's blinders limit his view to an isolated capitalist firm, since a view of the entire economy reveals that the capital of one capitalist is the material receptacle of the labor alienated to another capitalist. However, though the Trinity formula does not convince, it does accomplish the task of obfuscation by shifting the subject of the question: instead of asking why the activity of people under capitalism takes the form of wage-labor, potential analysts of capitalist daily life are transformed into academic house-Marxists who ask whether or not labor is the only "factor of production."

Thus Economics (and capitalist ideology in general) treats land, money, and the products of labor, as things which have the power to produce, to create value, to work for their owners, to transform the world. This is what Marx called the *fetishism* which characterizes people's everyday conceptions, and which is raised to the level of dogma by Economics. For the economist, living people are *things* ("factors of production"), and things *live* (money "works," Capital "produces").

The fetish worshipper attributes the product of his own activity to his fetish. As a result, he ceases to exert his own power (the power to transform nature, the power to determine the form and content of his daily life); he exerts only those "powers" which he attributes to his fetish (the "power" to buy commodities). In other words, the fetish worshipper emasculates himself and attributes virility to his fetish.

But the fetish is a dead thing, not a living being; it has no virility. The fetish is no more than a thing for which, and through which, capitalist relations are maintained. The mysterious power of Capital, its "power" to produce, its virility, does not reside in itself, but in the fact that people alienate their creative activity, that they sell their labor to capitalists, that they materialize or reify their alienated labor in commodities. In other words, people are bought with the products of their own activity, yet they see their own activity as the activity of Capital, and their own products as the products of Capital. By attributing creative power to Capital and not to their own activity, they renounce their living activity, their everyday life, to Capital, which means that people *give themselves,* daily, to the personification of Capital, the capitalist.

By selling their labor, by alienating their activity, people daily reproduce the personifications of the dominant forms of activity under capitalism, they reproduce the wage-laborer and the capitalist. They do not merely reproduce the individuals physically, but socially as well; they reproduce individuals who are sellers of labor-power, and individuals who are owners of means of production; they reproduce the individuals as well as the specific activities, the sale as well as the ownership.

Every time people perform an activity they have not themselves defined and do not control, every time they pay for goods they produced with money they received in exchange for their alienated activity, every time they passively admire the products of their own activity as alien objects procured by their money, they give new life to Capital and annihilate their own lives.

The aim of the process is the reproduction of the relation between the worker and the capitalist. However, this is not the aim of the individual agents engaged in it. Their activities are not transparent to them; their eyes are fixed on the *fetish* that stands between the act and its result. The individual agents keep their eyes fixed on *things,* precisely those things for which capitalist relations are established. The worker as producer aims to exchange his daily labor for money-wages, he aims precisely for the thing through which his relation to the capitalist is re-established, the thing through which he reproduces himself as a wage-worker and the other as a capitalist. The worker as consumer exchanges his money for products of labor, precisely the things which the capitalist has to sell in order to realize his Capital.

The daily transformation of living activity into Capital is *mediated* by things, it is not *carried out by* the things. The fetish worshipper does not know this; for him labor and land, instruments and money, entrepreneurs and bankers, are all "factors" and "agents." When a hunter wearing an amulet downs a deer with a stone, he may consider the amulet an essential "factor" in downing the deer and even in providing the deer as an object to be downed. If he is a responsible and well-educated fetish worshipper, he will devote his attention to his amulet, nourishing it with care and admiration; in order to improve the material conditions of his life, he will improve the way he wears his fetish, not the way he throws the stone; in a bind, he may even send his amulet to "hunt" for him. His own daily activities are not transparent to him: when he eats well, he fails to see that it is his own action of throwing the stone, and not the action of the amulet, that provided his food; when he starves, he fails to see that it is his own action of worshipping the amulet instead of hunting, and not the wrath of his fetish, that causes his starvation.

The fetishism of commodities and money, the mystification of one's own daily activities, the religion of everyday life which attributes living activity to inanimate things, is not a mental caprice born in men's imaginations; it has its origin in the character of social relations under capitalism. Men do in fact relate to each other through things; the fetish is in fact the occasion for which they act collectively, and through which they reproduce their activity. But it is not the fetish that performs the activity. It is not Capital that transforms raw materials, nor Capital that produces goods. If living activity did not transform the materials, these would remain untransformed, inert, dead matter. If men were not disposed to continue selling their living activity, the impotence of Capital would be revealed; Capital would cease to exist; its last remaining potency would be the power to remind people of a bypassed form of everyday life characterized by daily universal prostitution.

The worker alienates his life in order to preserve his life. If he did not sell his living activity he would not get a wage and could not survive. However, it is not the wage that makes alienation the condition for survival. If men were collectively not disposed to sell their lives, if they were disposed to take control over their own activities, universal prostitution would not be a condition for survival. It is people's disposition to continue selling their labor, and not the *things* for which they sell it, that makes the alienation of living activity necessary for the preservation of life.

The living activity sold by the worker is bought by the capitalist. And it is only this living activity that breathes life into Capital and makes it "productive." The capitalist, an "owner" of raw materials and instruments of production, presents natural objects and products of other people's labor as his own "private property." But it is not the mysterious power of Capital that creates the capitalist's "private property"; living activity is what creates the "property," and the form of that activity is what keeps it "private."

Transformation of Living Activity into Capital

The transformation of living activity into Capital takes place *through* things, daily, but is not carried out *by* things. Things which are products of human activity *seem* to be active agents because activities and contacts are established for and through things, and because people's activities are not transparent to them; they confuse the mediating object with the cause.

In the capitalist process of production, the worker embodies or materializes his alienated living energy in an inert object by using instruments which are embodiments of other people's activity. (Sophisticated industrial instruments embody the intellectual and manual activity of countless generations of inventors, improvers and producers from all corners of the globe and from varied forms of society.) The instruments in themselves are inert objects; they are material embodiments of living activity, but are not themselves alive. The only active agent in the production process is the living laborer. He uses the products of other people's labor and infuses them with life, so to speak, but the life is his own; he is not able to resurrect the individuals who stored their living activity in his instrument. The instrument may enable him to do more during a given time period, and in this sense it may raise his productivity. But only the living labor which is able to produce can be productive.

For example, when an industrial worker runs an electric lathe, he uses products of the labor of generations of physicists, inventors, electrical engineers, lathe makers. He is obviously more productive than a craftsman who carves the same object by hand. But it is in no sense the "Capital" at the disposal of the industrial worker which is more "productive" than the "Capital" of the craftsman. If generations of intellectual and manual activity had not been embodied in the electric lathe, if the industrial worker had to invent the lathe, electricity, and the electric lathe, then it would take him numerous lifetimes to turn a single object on an electric lathe, and no amount of Capital could raise his productivity above that of the craftsman who carves the object by hand.

The notion of the "productivity of capital," and particularly the detailed measurement of that "productivity," are inventions of the "science" of Economics, that religion of capitalist daily life which uses up people's energy in the worship, admiration and flattery of the central fetish of capitalist society. Medieval colleagues of these "scientists" performed detailed measurements of the height and width of angels in Heaven, without ever asking what angels or Heaven were, and taking for granted the existence of both.

The result of the worker's sold activity is a product which does not belong to him. This product is an embodiment of his labor, a materialization of a part of his life, a receptacle which contains his living activity, but it is not his; it is as alien to him as his labor. He did not decide to make it, and when it is made he does not dispose of it. If he wants it, he has to buy it. What he has made is not simply a product with certain useful properties; for that he did not need to sell his labor to a capitalist in exchange for a wage; he need only have picked the necessary materials and the available tools, he need only have shaped the materials guided by his goals and limited by his knowledge and ability. (It is obvious that an individual can only do this marginally; men's appropriation and use of the materials and tools available to them can only take place after the overthrow of the capitalist form of activity.)

What the worker produces under capitalist conditions is a product with a very specific property, the property of salability. What his alienated activity produces is a *commodity*.

Because capitalist production is commodity production, the statement that the goal of the process is the satisfaction of human needs is false; it is a rationalization and an apology. The "satisfaction of human needs" is not the goal of the capitalist or of the worker engaged in production, nor is it a result of the process. The worker sells his labor in order to get a wage; the specific content of the labor is indifferent to him; he does not alienate his labor to a capitalist who does not give him a wage in exchange for it, no matter how many human needs this capitalist's products may satisfy. The capitalist buys labor and engages it in production in order to emerge with commodities which can be sold. He is indifferent to the specific properties of the product, just as he is indifferent to people's needs; all that interests him about the product is how much it will sell for, and all that interests him about people's needs is how much they "need" to buy and how they can be coerced, through propaganda and psychological conditioning, to "need" more. The capitalist's goal is to satisfy *his* need to reproduce and enlarge Capital, and the result of the process is the expanded reproduction of wage labor and Capital (which are not "human needs").

The commodity produced by the worker is exchanged by the capitalist for a specific quantity of money; the commodity is a *value* which is exchanged for an equivalent *value*. In other words, the living and past labor materialized in the product can exist in two distinct yet equivalent forms, in commodities and in money, or in what is common to both, *value*. This does not mean that value is labor. Value is the social *form* of reified (materialized) labor in capitalist society.

Under capitalism, social relations are not established directly; they are established through value. Everyday activity is not exchanged directly; it is exchanged *in the form of value*. Consequently, what happens to living activity under capitalism cannot be traced by observing the activity itself, but only by following the metamorphoses of value.

When the living activity of people takes the form of *labor* (alienated activity), it acquires the property of exchangeability; it acquires the form of value. In other words, the labor can be exchanged for an "equivalent" quantity of money (wages). The deliberate alienation of living activity, which is perceived as necessary for survival by the members of capitalist society, itself reproduces the capitalist form within which alienation is necessary for survival. Because of the fact that living activity has the form of value, the products of that activity must also have the form of value: they must be exchangeable for money. This is obvious since, if the products of labor did not take the form of value, but for example the form of useful objects at the disposal of society, then they would either remain in the factory or they would be taken freely by the members of society whenever a need for them arose; in either case, the money-wages received by the workers would have no *value*, and living activity could not be *sold* for an "equivalent" quantity of money; living activity could not be alienated. Consequently, as soon as living activity takes the form of value, the products of that activity take the form of value, and the reproduction of everyday life takes place through changes or metamorphoses of value.

The capitalist sells the products of labor on a market; he exchanges them for an equivalent sum of money; he realizes a determined value.

The specific magnitude of this value on a particular market is the *price* of the commodities. For the academic Economist, Price is St. Peter's key to the gates of Heaven. Like Capital itself, Price moves within a wonderful world which consists entirely of objects; the objects have human relations with each other, and are alive; they transform each other, communicate with each other; they marry and have children. And of course it is only through the grace of these intelligent, powerful and creative objects that people can be so happy in capitalist society.

In the Economist's pictorial representations of the workings of Heaven, the angels do everything and men do nothing at all; men simply enjoy what these superior beings do for them. Not only does Capital produce and money work; other mysterious beings have similar virtues. Thus Supply, a quantity of things which are sold, and Demand, a quantity of things which are bought, together determine Price, a quantity of money; when Supply and Demand marry on a particular point of the diagram, they give birth to Equilibrium Price, which corresponds to a universal state of bliss. The activities of everyday life are played out by things, and people are reduced to things ("factors of production") during their "productive" hours, and to passive spectators of things during their "leisure time." The virtue of the Economic Scientist consists of his ability to attribute the outcome of people's everyday activities to things, and of his inability to see the living activity of people underneath the antics of the things. For the Economist, the things *through* which the activity of people is regulated under capitalism are themselves the mothers and sons, the causes and consequences of their own activity.

The magnitude of value, namely the price of a commodity, the quantity of money for which it exchanges, is not determined by things, but by the daily activities of people. Supply and demand, perfect and imperfect competition, are nothing more than social forms of products and activities in capitalist society; they have no life of their own. The fact that activity is alienated, namely that labor-time is sold for a specific sum of money, that it has a certain value, has several consequences for the magnitude of the value of the products of that labor. The value of the sold commodities must *at least* be equal to the value of the labor-time. This is obvious both from the standpoint of the individual capitalist firm, and from the standpoint of society as a whole. If the value of the commodities sold by the individual capitalist were smaller than the value of the labor he hired, then his labor expenditures alone would be larger than his earnings, and he would quickly go bankrupt. Socially, if the value of the laborers' production were smaller than the value of their consumption, then the labor force could not even reproduce itself, not to speak of a class of capitalists. However, if the value of the commodities were merely equal to the value of the labor-time expended on them, the commodity producers would merely reproduce themselves, and their society would not be a capitalist society; their activity might still consist of commodity production, but it would not be capitalist commodity production.

For labor to create Capital, the value of the products of labor must be larger than the value of the labor. In other words, the labor force must produce a *surplus product,* a quantity of goods which it does not consume, and this surplus product must be transformed into *surplus value,* a form of value which is not appropriated by workers as wages, but by capitalists as profit. Furthermore, the value of the products of labor must be larger still, since living labor is not the only kind of labor materialized in them. In the production process, workers expend their own energy, but they also use up the stored labor of others as instruments, and they shape materials on which labor was previously expended.

This leads to the strange result that the value of the laborer's products and the value of his wage are different magnitudes, namely that the sum of money received by the capitalist when he sells the commodities produced by his hired laborers is different from the sum he pays the laborers. This difference is not explained by the fact that the used-up materials and tools must be paid for. If the value of the sold commodities were equal to the value of the living labor and the instruments, there would still be no room for capitalists. The fact is that the difference between the two magnitudes must be large enough to support a class of capitalists—not only the individuals, but also the specific activity that these individuals engage in, namely the purchase of labor. The difference between the total value of the products and the value of the labor spent on their production is surplus value, the seed of Capital.

In order to locate the origin of surplus value, it is necessary to examine why the value of the labor is smaller than the value of the commodities produced by it. The alienated activity of the worker transforms materials with the aid of instruments, and produces a certain quantity of commodities. However, when these commodities are sold and the used-up materials and instruments are paid for, the workers are not given the remaining value of their products as their wages; they are given less. In other words, during every working day, the workers perform a certain quantity of unpaid labor, *forced labor,* for which they receive no equivalent.

The performance of this unpaid labor, this forced labor, is another "condition for survival" in capitalist society. However, like alienation, this condition is not imposed by nature, but by the collective practice of people, by their everyday activities. Before the existence of unions, an individual worker accepted whatever forced labor was available, since rejection of the labor would have meant that other workers would accept the available terms of exchange, and the individual worker would receive no wage. Workers competed with each other for the wages offered by capitalists; if a worker quit because the wage was unacceptably low, an unemployed worker was willing to replace him, since for the unemployed a small wage is higher than no wage at all. This competition among workers was called "free labor" by capitalists, who made great sacrifices to maintain the freedom of workers, since it was precisely this freedom that preserved the surplus value of the capitalist and made it possible for him to accumulate Capital. It was not any worker's aim to produce more goods than he was paid for. His aim was to get a wage which was as large as possible. However, the existence of workers who got no wage at all, and whose conception of a large wage was consequently more modest than that of an employed worker, made it possible for the capitalist to hire labor at a lower wage. In fact, the existence of unemployed workers made it possible for the capitalist to pay the lowest wage that workers were willing to work for. Thus the result of the collective daily activity of the workers, each striving individually for the largest possible wage, was to lower the wages of all; the effect of the competition of each against all was that all got the smallest possible wage, and the capitalist got the largest possible surplus.

The daily practice of all annuls the goals of each. But the workers did not know that their situation was a product of their own daily behavior; their own activities were not transparent to them. To the workers it seemed that low wages were simply a natural part of life, like illness and death, and that falling wages were a natural catastrophe, like a flood or a hard winter. The critiques of socialists and the analyses of Marx, as well as an increase in industrial development which afforded more time for reflection, stripped away some of the veils and made it possible for workers to see through their activities to some extent. However, in Western Europe and the United States, workers did not get rid of the capitalist form of daily life; they formed unions. And in the different material conditions of the Soviet Union and Eastern Europe, workers (and peasants) replaced the capitalist class with a state bureaucracy that purchases alienated labor and accumulates Capital in the name of Marx.

With unions, daily life is similar to what it was before unions. In fact, it is almost the same. Daily life continues to consist of labor, of alienated activity, and of unpaid labor, or forced labor. The unionized worker no longer settles the terms of his alienation; union functionaries do this for him. The terms on which the worker's activity is alienated are no longer guided by the individual worker's need to accept what is available; they are now guided by the union bureaucrat's need to maintain his position as pimp between the sellers of labor and the buyers.

With or without unions, surplus value is neither a product of nature nor of Capital; it is created by the daily activities of people. In the performance of their daily activities, people are not only disposed to alienate these activities, they are also disposed to reproduce the conditions which force them to alienate their activities, to reproduce Capital and thus the power of Capital to purchase labor. This is not because they do not know "what the alternative is." A person who is incapacitated by chronic indigestion because he eats too much grease does not continue eating grease because he does not know what the alternative is. Either he prefers being incapacitated to giving up grease, or else it is not clear to him that his daily consumption of grease causes his incapacity. And if his doctor, preacher, teacher and politician tell him, first, that the grease is what keeps him alive, and secondly that they already do for him everything he would do if he were well, then it is not surprising that his activity is not transparent to him and that he makes no great effort to render it transparent.

The production of surplus value is a condition of survival, not for the population, but for the capitalist system. Surplus value is the portion of the value of commodities produced by labor which is not returned to the laborers. It can be expressed either in commodities or in money (just as Capital can be expressed either as a quantity of things or of money), but this does not alter the fact that it is an expression for the materialized labor which is stored in a given quantity of products. Since the products can be exchanged for an "equivalent" quantity of money, the money "stands for," or represents, the same value as the products. The money can, in turn, be exchanged for another quantity of products of "equivalent" value. The ensemble of these exchanges, which take place simultaneously during the performance of capitalist daily life, constitutes the capitalist process of circulation. It is through this process that the metamorphosis of surplus value into Capital takes place.

The portion of value which does not return to labor, namely surplus value, allows the capitalist to exist, and it also allows him to do much more than simply exist. The capitalist invests a portion of this surplus value; he hires new workers and buys new means of production; he expands his dominion. What this means is that the capitalist *accumulates new labor*, both in the form of the living labor he hires and of the past labor (paid and unpaid) which is stored in the materials and machines he buys.

The capitalist class as a whole accumulates the surplus labor of society, but this process takes place on a social scale and consequently cannot be seen if one observes only the activities of an individual capitalist. It must be remembered that the products bought by a given capitalist as instruments have the same characteristics as the products he sells. A first capitalist sells instruments to a second capitalist for a given sum of value, and only a part of this value is returned to workers as wages; the remaining part is surplus value, with which the first capitalist buys new instruments and labor. The second capitalist buys the instruments for the given value, which means that he pays for the total quantity of labor rendered to the first capitalist, the quantity of labor which was remunerated as well as the quantity performed free of charge. This means that the instruments accumulated by the second capitalist contain the unpaid labor performed for the first. The second capitalist, in turn, sells his products for a given value, and returns only a portion of this value to his laborers; he uses the remainder for new instruments and labor.

If the whole process were squeezed into a single time period, and if all the capitalists were aggregated into one, it would be seen that the value with which the capitalist acquires new instruments and labor is equal to the value of the products which he did not return to the producers. This accumulated surplus labor is *Capital*.

In terms of capitalist society as a whole, the total Capital is equal to the sum of unpaid labor performed by generations of human beings whose lives consisted of the daily alienation of their living activity. In other words Capital, in the face of which men sell their living days, is the product of the sold activity of men, and is reproduced and expanded every day a man sells another working day, every moment he decides to continue living the capitalist form of daily life.

Storage and Accumulation of Human Activity

The transformation of surplus labor into Capital is a specific historical form of a more general process, the process of industrialization, the permanent transformation of man's material environment.

Certain essential characteristics of this consequence of human activity under capitalism can be grasped by means of a simplified illustration. In an imaginary society, people spend most of their active time producing food and other necessities; only part of their time is "surplus time" in the sense that it is exempted from the production of necessities. This surplus activity may be devoted to the production of food for priests and warriors who do not them-selves produce; it may be used to produce goods which are burned for sacred occasions; it may be used up in the performance of cer-emonies or gymnastic exercises. In any of these cases, the material conditions of these people are not likely to change, from one genera-tion to another, as a result of their daily activities. However, one generation of people of this imaginary society may store their surplus time instead of using it up. For example, they may spend this surplus time winding up springs. The next generation may unwind the energy stored in the springs to perform necessary tasks, or may simply use the energy of the springs to wind new springs. In either case, the stored surplus labor of the earlier generation will provide the new generation with a larger quantity of surplus working time. The new generation may also store this surplus in springs and in other re-ceptacles. In a relatively short period, the labor stored in the springs will exceed the labor time available to any living generation; with the expenditure of relatively little energy, the people of this imaginary society will be able to harness the springs to most of their necessary tasks, and also to the task of winding new springs for coming generations. Most of the living hours which they previously spent producing necessities will now be available for activities which are not dictated by necessity but projected by the imagination.

At first glance it seems unlikely that people would devote living hours to the bizarre task of winding springs. It seems just as un-likely, even if they wound the springs, that they would store them for future generations, since the unwinding of the springs might provide, for example, a marvelous spectacle on festive days.

However, if people did not dispose of their own lives, if their working activity were not their own, if their practical activity con-sisted of *forced labor,* then human activity might well be harnessed to the task of winding springs, the task of storing surplus working time in material receptacles. The historical role of Capitalism, a role which was performed by people who accepted the legitimacy of others to dispose of their lives, consisted precisely of storing human activity in material receptacles by means of forced labor.

As soon as people submit to the "power" of money to buy stored labor as well as living activity, as soon as they accept the fictional "right" of money-holders to control and dispose of the stored as well as the living activity of society, they transform money into Capital and the owners of money into Capitalists.

This double alienation, the alienation of living activity in the form of wage labor, and the alienation of the activity of past genera-tions in the form of stored labor (means of production), is not a single act which took place sometime in history. The relation between workers and capitalists is not a thing which imposed itself on society at some point in the past, once and for all. At no time did men sign a contract, or even make a verbal agreement, in which they gave up the power over their living activity, and in which they gave up the power over the living activity of all future generations on all parts of the globe.

Capital wears the mask of a natural force; it seems as solid as the earth itself; its movements appear as irreversible as tides; its crises seem as unavoidable as earthquakes and floods. Even when it is admitted that the power of Capital is created by men, this admission may merely be the occasion for the invention of an even more imposing mask, the mask of a man-made force, a Frankenstein monster, whose power inspires more awe than that of any natural force.

However, Capital is neither a natural force nor a man-made monster which was created sometime in the past and which dominated human life ever since.

The power of Capital does not reside in money, since money is a social convention which has no more "power" than men are willing to grant it; when men refuse to sell their labor, money cannot perform even the simplest tasks, because money does not "work."

Nor does the power of Capital reside in the material receptacles in which the labor of past generations is stored, since the potential energy stored in these receptacles can be liberated by the activity of living people whether or not the receptacles are Capital, namely alien "property." Without living activity, the collection of objects which constitute society's Capital would merely be a scattered heap of assorted artifacts with no life of their own, and the "owners" of Capital would merely be a scattered assortment of uncommonly uncreative people (by training) who surround themselves with bits of paper in a vain attempt to resuscitate memories of past grandeur. The only "power" of Capital resides in the daily activities of living people; this "power" consists of the disposition of people to sell their daily activities in exchange for money, and to give up control over the products of their own activity and of the activity of earlier generations.

As soon as a person sells his labor to a capitalist and accepts only a part of his product as payment for that labor, he creates conditions for the purchase and exploitation of other people. No man would willingly give his arm or his child in exchange for money; yet when a man deliberately and consciously sells his working life in order to acquire the necessities for life, he not only reproduces the conditions which continue to make the sale of his life a necessity for its preservation; he also creates conditions which make the sale of life a necessity for other people. Later generations may of course refuse to sell their working lives for the same reason that he refused to sell his arm; however each failure to refuse alienated and forced labor enlarges the stock of stored labor with which Capital can buy working lives.

In order to transform surplus labor into Capital, the capitalist has to find a way to store it in material receptacles, in new means of production, and he must hire new laborers to activate the new means of production. In other words, he must enlarge his enterprise, or start a new enterprise in a different branch of production. This presupposes or requires the existence of materials that can be shaped into new salable commodities, the existence of buyers of the new products, and the existence of people who are poor enough to be willing to sell their labor. These requirements are themselves created by capitalist activity, and capitalists recognize no limits or obstacles to their activity; the democracy of Capital demands absolute freedom.

Imperialism is not merely the "last stage" of Capitalism; it is also the first.

Anything which can be transformed into a marketable good is grist for Capital's mill, whether it lies on the capitalist's land or on the neighbor's, whether it lies above ground or under, floats on the sea or crawls on its floor; whether it is confined to other continents or other planets. All of humanity's explorations of nature, from Alchemy to Physics, are mobilized to search for new materials in which to store labor, to find new objects that someone can be taught to buy.

Buyers for old and new products are created by any and all available means, and new means are constantly discovered. "Open markets" and "open doors" are established by force and fraud. If people lack the means to buy the capitalists' products, they are hired by capitalists and are paid for producing the goods they wish to buy; if local craftsmen already produce what the capitalists have to sell, the craftsmen are ruined or bought-out; if laws or traditions ban the use of certain products, the laws and the traditions are destroyed; if people lack the objects on which to use the capitalists' products, they are taught to buy these objects; if people run out of physical or biological wants, then capitalists "satisfy" their "spiritual wants" and hire psychologists to create them; if people are so satiated with the products of capitalists that they can no longer use new objects, they are taught to buy objects and spectacles which have no use but can simply be observed and admired.

Poor people are found in pre-agrarian and agrarian societies on every continent; if they are not poor enough to be willing to sell their labor when the capitalists arrive, they are impoverished by the activities of the capitalists themselves. The lands of hunters gradually

48

become the "private property" of "owners" who use state violence to restrict the hunters to "reservations" which do not contain enough food to keep them alive. The tools of peasants gradually become available only from the same merchant who generously lends them the money with which to buy the tools, until the peasants' "debts" are so large that they are forced to sell land which neither they nor any of their ancestors had ever bought. The buyers of craftsmen's products gradually become reduced to the merchants who market the products, until the day comes when a merchant decides to house "his craftsmen" under the same roof, and provides them with the instruments which will enable all of them to concentrate their activity on the production of the most profitable items. Independent as well as dependent hunters, peasants and craftsmen, free men as well as slaves, are transformed into hired laborers. Those who previously disposed of their own lives in the face of harsh material conditions cease to dispose of their own lives precisely when they take up the task of modifying their material conditions; those who were previously conscious creators of their own meager existence become unconscious victims of their own activity even while abolishing the meagerness of their existence. Men who were much but had little now have much but are little.

The production of new commodities, the "opening" of new markets, the creation of new workers, are not three separate activities; they are three aspects of the same activity. A new labor force is created precisely in order to produce the new commodities; the wages received by these laborers are themselves the new market; their unpaid labor is the source of new expansion. Neither natural nor cultural barriers halt the spread of Capital, the transformation of people's daily activity into alienated labor, the transformation of their surplus labor into the "private property" of capitalists. However, Capital is not a natural force; it is a set of activities performed by people every day; it is a form of daily life; its continued existence and expansion presuppose only one essential condition: the disposition of people to continue to alienate their working lives and thus reproduce the capitalist form of daily life.

1969

Revolt in Socialist Yugoslavia

"Heretics are always more dangerous than enemies," concluded a Yugoslav philosopher after analyzing the repression of Marxist intellectuals by the Marxist regime of Poland. (S. Stojanović, in *Student*, Belgrade, April 9, 1968, p. 7.)

In Yugoslavia, where "workers' self-management" has become the official ideology, a new struggle for popular control has exposed the gap between the official ideology and the social relations which it claims to describe. The heretics who exposed this gap have been temporarily isolated; their struggle has been momentarily suppressed. The ideology of "self-management" continues to serve as a mask for a commercial-technocratic bureaucracy which has successfully concentrated the wealth and power created by the Yugoslav working population. However, even a single and partial removal of the mask spoils its efficacy: the ruling "elite" of Yugoslavia has been exposed; its "Marxist" proclamations have been unveiled as myths which, once unveiled, no longer serve to justify its rule.

In June 1968, the gap between theory and practice, between official proclamations and social relations, was exposed through practice, through social activity: students began to organize themselves in demonstrations and general assemblies, and the regime which proclaims self-management reacted to this rare example of popular self-organization by putting an end to it through police and press repression.

The nature of the gap between Yugoslav ideology and society had been analyzed before June 1968, not by "class enemies" of Yugoslavia's ruling "revolutionary Marxists," but by Yugoslav revolutionary Marxists—by heretics. According to official declarations, in a society where the working class is already in power there are no strikes, because it is absurd for workers to strike against themselves. Yet strikes, which were not reported by the press because they could not take place in Yugoslavia, have been breaking out for the past eleven years— and massively (*Susret*, No. 98, April 18, 1969). Furthermore, "strikes in Yugoslavia represent a symptom of the attempt to revive the workers' movement." In other words, in a society where workers are said to rule, the workers' movement is dead. "This may sound paradoxical to some people. But it is no paradox due to the fact that workers' self-management exists largely 'on paper'. . ." (L. Tadić in *Student*, April 9, 1968, p. 7.)

Against whom do students demonstrate, against whom do workers strike, in a society where students and workers already govern themselves? The answer to this question cannot be found in declarations of the Yugoslav League of Communists, but only in critical analyses of Yugoslav social relations—analyses which are heretical because they contradict the official declarations. In capitalist societies, activities are

50

justified in the name of progress and the national interest. In Yugoslav society, programs, policies and reforms are justified in the name of progress and the working class. However, it is not the workers who initiate the dominant projects , nor do the projects serve the workers' interests: "On the one hand, sections of the working class are wage-workers who live below the level necessary for existence. The burden of the economic reform is carried by the working class, a fact which must be openly admitted. On the other hand, small groups unscrupulously capitalize themselves overnight, on the basis of private labor, services, commerce, and as middlemen. Their capital is not based on their labor, but on speculation, mediation, transformation of personal labor into property relations, and often on outright corruption." (M. Pečujlić in *Student,* April 30, 1968, p. 2.)

The paradox can be stated in more general terms: social relations already known to Marx reappear in a society which has experienced a socialist revolution led by a Marxist party in the name of the working class. Workers receive wages in exchange for their sold labor (even if the wages are called "personal incomes" and "bonuses"); the wages are an equivalent for the material goods necessary for the workers' physical and social survival; the surplus labor, appropriated by state or enterprise bureaucracies and transformed into capital, returns as an alien force which determines the material and social conditions of the workers' existence. According to official histories, Yugoslavia eliminated exploitation in 1945, when the Yugoslav League of Communists won state power. Yet workers whose surplus labor supports a state or commercial bureaucracy, whose unpaid labor turns against them as a force which does not seem to result from their own activity but from some higher power—such workers perform forced labor: they are exploited. According to official histories, Yugoslavia eliminated the bureaucracy as a social group over the working class in 1952, when the system of workers' self-management was introduced. But workers who alienate their living activity in exchange for the means of life do not control themselves; they are controled by those to whom they alienate their labor and its products, even if these people eliminated themselves in legal documents and proclamations.

In the United States, trusts ceased to exist legally precisely at the point in history when trusts began to centralize the enormous productive power of the U.S. working class. In Yugoslavia, the social stratum which manages the working class ceased to exist in 1952. But in actual fact, "the dismantling of the unified centralized bureaucratic monopoly led to a net of self-managing institutions in all branches of social activity (nets of workers' councils, self-managing bodies, etc.) From a formal-legal, normative, institutional point of view, the society is self-managed. But is this also the status of real relations? Behind the self-managed façade, within the self-managed bodies, two powerful and opposed tendencies arise from the production relations. Inside of each center of decision there is a bureaucracy in a metamorphosed, decentralized form.

It consists of informal groups who maintain a monopoly in the management of labor, a monopoly in the distribution of surplus labor against the workers and their interests, who appropriate on the basis of their position in the bureaucratic hierarchy and not on the basis of labor, who try to keep the representatives of 'their' organization, of 'their' region, permanently in power so as to ensure their own position and to maintain the former separation, the unqualified labor and the irrational production—transferring the burden to the workers. Among themselves they behave like the representatives of monopoly ownership. . . On the other hand, there is a profoundly socialist, self-governing tendency, a movement which has already begun to stir. . ." (Pečujlić in *Ibid.*)

This profoundly socialist tendency represents a struggle against the dependence and helplessness which allows workers to be exploited with the products of their own labor; it represents a struggle for control of all social activities by those who perform them. Yet what form can this struggle take in a society which already proclaims self-organization and self-control as its social, economic and legal system? What forms of revolutionary struggle can be developed in a context where a communist party already holds state power, and where this communist party has already proclaimed the end of bureaucratic rule and raised self-management to the level of an official ideology? The struggle, clearly, cannot consist of the expropriation of the capitalist class, since this expropriation has already taken place; nor can the struggle consist of the taking of state power by a revolutionary Marxist party, since such a party has already wielded state power for a quarter of a century. It is of course possible to do the thing over again, and to convince oneself that the outcome will be better the second time than the first. But the political imagination is not so poor that it need limit its perspectives to past failures. It is today realized, in Yugoslavia as elsewhere, that the expropriation of the capitalist class and its replacement by "the organization of the working class" (i.e. the Communist Party), that the taking of national-state power by "the organization of the working class" and even the official proclamation of various types of "socialism" by the Communist Party in power, are already historical realities, and that they have not meant the end of commodity production, alienated labor, forced labor, nor the beginning of popular self-organization and self-control.

Consequently, forms of organized struggle which have already proved themselves efficient instruments for the acceleration of industrialization and for rationalizing social relations in terms of the model of the Brave New World, cannot be the forms of organization of a struggle for independent and critical initiative and control on the part of the entire working population. The taking of state power by the bureaucracy of a political party is nothing more than what the words say, even if this party calls itself "the organization of the working class," and even if it calls its own rule "the Dictatorship of the Proletariat" or "Workers'

Self-Management." Furthermore, Yugoslav experience does not even show that the taking of state power by the "organization of the working class" is a stage on the way toward workers' control of social production, or even that the official proclamation of "workers' self-management" is a stage towards its realization. The Yugoslav experiment would represent such a stage, at least historically, only in case Yugoslav workers were the first in the world to initiate a successful struggle for the de-alienation of power at all levels of social life. However, Yugoslav workers have not initiated such a struggle. As in capitalist societies, students have initiated such a struggle, and Yugoslav students were not among the first.

The conquest of state power by a political party which uses a Marxist vocabulary in order to manipulate the working class must be distinguished from another, very different historical task: the overthrow of commodity relations and the establishment of socialist relations. For over half a century, the former has been presented in the guise of the latter. The rise of a "new left" has put an end to this confusion; the revolutionary movement which is experiencing a revival on a world scale is characterized precisely by its refusal to push a party bureaucracy into state power, and by its opposition to such a bureaucracy where it is already in power.

Party ideologues argue that the "new left" in capitalist societies has nothing in common with student revolts in "socialist countries." Such a view, at best, is exaggerated: with respect to Yugoslavia it can at most be said that the Yugoslav student movement is not as highly developed as in some capitalist countries: until June, 1968, Yugoslav students were known for their political passivity, pro-United States sympathies and petit-bourgeois life goals. However, despite the wishes of the ideologues, Yugoslav students have not remained far behind; the search for new forms of organization adequate for the tasks of socialist revolution has not remained alien to Yugoslav students. In May, 1968, while a vast struggle to de-alienate all forms of separate social power was gaining historical experience in France, the topic "Students and Politics" was discussed at the Belgrade Faculty of Law. The "theme which set the tone of the discussion" was: ". . . the possibility for human engagement in the 'new left' movement which, in the words of Dr. S. Stojanović, opposes the mythology of the 'welfare state' with its classical bourgeois democracy, and also the classical left parties—the social-democratic parties which have succeeded by all possible means in blunting revolutionary goals in developed Western societies, as well as the communist parties which often discredited the original ideals for which they fought, frequently losing them altogether in remarkably bureaucratic deformations." ("The Topic is Action," *Student,*May 14, 1968, p. 4.)

By May, 1968, Yugoslav students had a great deal in common with their comrades in capitalist societies. A front page editorial of the Belgrade student newspaper said, "the tension of the present social-political situation is made more acute by the fact that there are no quick

53

and easy solutions to numerous problems. Various forms of tension are visible in the University, and the lack of perspectives, the lack of solutions to numerous problems, is at the root of various forms of behavior. Feeling this, many are asking if the tension might be transformed into conflict, into a serious political crisis, and what form this crisis will take. Some think the crisis cannot be avoided, but can only be blunted, because there is no quick and efficient way to affect conditions which characterize the entire social structure, and which are the direct causes of the entire situation." ("Signs of Political Crisis,"*Student* , May 21, 1968, p. 1.) The same front page of the student paper carried the following quotation from Marx, on "the veiled alienation at the heart of labor": ". . . Labor produces wonders for the rich, but misery for the worker. It produces palaces, but a hovel for the worker. It produces beauty, but horror for the worker. It replaces labor with machines, but throws part of the workers backward into barbarian work, and transforms the other part into machines. It produces spirit, but for the worker it produces stupidity and cretinism."

The same month, the editorial of the Belgrade Youth Federation journal said, " . . . the revolutionary role of Yugoslav students, in our opinion, lies in their engagement to deal with **general social** problems and contradictions (among which the problems and contradictions of the social and material situation of students are included). Special student problems, no matter how drastic, **cannot** be solved in isolation, separate from the general social problems: the material situation of students cannot be separated from the economic situation of the society; student self-government cannot be separated from the social problems of self-government; the situation of the University from the situation of society. . . " (*Susret*, May 15, 1968). The following issue of the same publication contained a discussion on "the Conditions and the Content of Political Engagement for Youth Today" which included the following observation: "University reform is thus not possible without reform or, why not, revolutionizing of the entire society, because the university cannot be separated from the wider spectrum of social institutions. From this it follows that freedom of thought and action, namely autonomy for the University, is only possible if the entire society is transformed, and if thus transformed it makes possible a general climate of freedom and self-government." (*Susret*, June 1, 1968.)

* * *

In April, 1968, like their comrades in capitalist countries, Yugoslav students demonstrated their solidarity with the Vietnamese National Liberation Front and their opposition to United States militarism. When Rudi Dutschke was shot in Berlin as a consequence of the Springer Press campaign against radical West German students, Yugoslav students demonstrated their solidarity with the German Socialist Student Federation (S.D.S.). The Belgrade student newspaper carried articles by Rudi

Dutschke and by the German Marxist philosopher Ernst Bloch. The experience of the world student movement was communicated to Yugoslav students. "Student revolts which have taken place in many countries this year have shown that youth are able to carry out important projects in the process of changing a society. It can be said that these revolts have influenced circles in our University, since it is obvious that courage and the will to struggle have increased, that the critical consciousness of numerous students has sharpened (revolution is often the topic of intellectual discussion)." (*Student*, April 23, 1968, p. 1.) As for the forms of organization through which this will to struggle could express itself, Paris provided an example. "What is completely new and extremely important in the new revolutionary movement of the Paris students—but also of German, Italian and U.S. students—is that the movement was possible only because it was independent of all existing political organizations. All of these organizations, including the Communist Party, have become part of the system; they have become integrated into the rules of the daily parliamentary game; they have hardly been willing to risk the positions they've already reached to throw themselves into this insanely courageous and at first glance hopeless operation." (M.Marković, *Student*, May 21, 1968.)

Another key element which contributed to the development of the Yugoslav student movement was the experience of Belgrade students with the bureaucracy of the student union. In April, students at the Philosophy Faculty composed a letter protesting the repression of Marxist intellectuals in Poland. "All over the world today, students are at the forefront in the struggle to create a human society, and thus we are profoundly surprised by the reactions of the Polish socialist regime. Free critical thought cannot be suppressed by any kind of power, not even by that which superficially leans on socialist ideals. For us, young Marxists, it is incomprehensible that today, in a socialist country, it is possible to tolerate anti-Semitic attacks and to use them for the solution of internal problems. We consider it unacceptable that after Polish socialism experienced so many painful experiences in the past, internal conflicts should be solved by such undemocratic means and that in their solution Marxist thought is persecuted. We also consider unscrupulous the attempts to separate and create conflict between the progressive student movement and the working class whose full emancipation is also the students' goal. . . " (*Student*, April 23, 1968, p. 4.) An assembly of students at the Philosophy Faculty sent this letter to Poland—and the University Board of the Yugoslav Student Union opposed the action. Why? The philosophy students themselves analyzed the function, and the interests, of their own bureaucracy: "The University Board of the Yugoslav Student Union was in a situation in which it had lost its political nerve, it could not react, it felt weak and did not feel any obligation to do something. Yet when this body was not asked, when its advice was not heard, action 'should not have been taken.' This is bad tactics and still worse respect for democracy which must come to

55

full expression in young people, like students. Precisely at the moment when the University Board had lost its understanding of the essence of the action, the discussion was channeled to the terrain of formalities: 'Whose opinion should have been sought?' 'Whose permission should have been gotten?' It wasn't asked who would begin an action in this atmosphere of passivity. Is it not paradoxical that the University Board turns against an action which was initiated precisely by its own members and not by any forum, if we keep in mind that the basic principle of our socialism is—**SELF-MANAGEMENT**, which means decision-making in the ranks of the members. In other words, our sin was that we applied our basic right of self-management. Organization can never be an end in itself, but only a means for the realization of ends. The greatest value of our action lies precisely in the fact that it was initiated by the rank and file, without directives or instructions from above, without crass institutionalized forms." (*Ibid.*)

With these elements—an awareness of the inseparability of university problems from the social relations of a society based on alienated labor, an awareness of the experience of the international "new left," and an awareness of the difference between self-organization by the rank and file and bureaucratic organization — the Belgrade students moved to action. The incident which set off the actions was minor. On the night of June 2, 1968, a performance which was to be held outdoors near the students' dormitories in New Belgrade, was held in a small room indoors; students who had come to see the performance could not get in. A spontaneous demonstration began, which soon included thousands of students; the demonstrators began to walk toward the government buildings. They were stopped, as in capitalist societies, by the police (who are officially called a "militia" in the self-managed language of Yugoslavia); students were beaten by militia batons; many were arrested.

The following day, June 3, continuous general assemblies were held in most of the faculties which compose the University of Belgrade (renamed The Red University *Karl Marx*), and also in the streets of New Belgrade. "In their talks students emphasized the gross social differen—tiation of Yugoslav society, the problem of unemployment, the increase of private property and the unearned wealth of one social layer, the unbearable condition of a large section of the working class and the need to carry out the principle of distribution according to labor consistently. The talks were interrupted by loud applause, by calls like *'Students with Workers,' 'We're sons of working people,' 'Down with the Socialist Bourgeoisie,' 'Freedom of the press and freedom to demonstrate!'* " (*Student*, special issue, June 4, 1968, p. 1.)

Police repression was followed by press repression. The Yugoslav (Communist) press did not communicate the students' struggle to the rest of the population. It communicated a struggle of students for student-problems, a struggle of a separate group for greater privileges, a struggle which had not taken place. The front page of the June 4 issue of *Student,* which was banned by Belgrade authorities, describes the attempt of the press to present a nascent revolutionary struggle as a student revolt for special privileges: "The press has once again succeeded in distorting the events at the University. . . According to the press, students are fighting to improve their own material conditions. Yet everyone who took part in the meetings and demonstrations knows very well that the students were already turned in another direction—toward a struggle which encompasses the general interests of our society, above all a struggle for the interests of the working class. This is why the announcements sent out by the demonstrators emphasized above all else the decrease of unjustified social differences. According to the students, this struggle (against social inequality) in addition to the struggle for relations of self-government and reform, is of central importance to the working class and to Yugoslavia today. The newspapers did not quote a single speaker who talked about unjustified social differences. . . The newspapers also omitted the main slogans called out during the meetings and demonstrations: *For the Unity of Workers and Students, Students with Workers,* and similar slogans which expressed a single idea and a single feeling: that the roads and interests of students are inseparable from those of the working class." (*Student,* June 4, 1968, p. 1.)

By June 5, The Yugoslav Student Federation had succeeded in gaining leadership over the growing movement, and in becoming its spokesman. The student organization proclaimed a "Political Action Program" which contained the revolutionary goals expressed by the students in the assemblies, meetings and demonstrations—but the program also contained, as if by way of an appendix, a "Part II" on "university reform." This appendix later played a key role in putting the newly awakened Yugoslav student movement back to sleep. Part I of the political action program emphasized social inequality first of all, unemployment, "democratization of all social and political organizations, particularly the League of Communists," the degeneration of social property into private property, speculation in housing, commercialization of culture. Yet Part II, which was probably not even read by radical students who were satisfied with the relatively accurate ex—pression of their goals in Part I, expresses a very different, in fact an opposite orientation. The first "demand" of Part II already presupposes that none of the goals expressed in Part I will be fulfilled: it is a demand for the adaptation of the university to the present requirements of the Yugoslav social system, namely a demand for technocratic reform which satisfies the requirements of Yugoslavia's commercial-technocratic regime: "Immediate reform of the school system to adapt it to the requirements of the social and cultural development of our economy and our self-management relations. . . " (*Student,* special issue, June 8, 1968, pp. 1-2.)

This crude reversal, this manipulation of the student revolt so as to make it serve the requirements of the dominant social relations against which the students had revolted, did not become evident until the following school year. The immediate reactions of the regime were far less subtle: they consisted of repression, isolation, separation. The forms of police repression included beatings and jailings, a ban on the student newspaper which carried the only complete report of the events, demonstrations and meetings, and on the night of June 6, "two agents of the secret police and a militia officer brutally attacked students distributing the student paper, grabbed 600 copies of the paper, tore them to pieces and burned them. All this took place in front of a large group of citizens who had gathered to receive copies of the paper." (*Student*, June 8, 1968, p. 3.)

In addition to police repression, the dominant interests succeeded in isolating and separating the students from the workers, they temporarily succeeded in their "unscrupulous attempt to separate and create conflict between the progressive student movement and the working class whose full emancipation is also the students' goal." This was done in numerous ways. The ban on the student press and mis-reporting by the official press kept workers ignorant of the students' goals; enterprise directors and their circles of experts "explained" the student struggle to "their" workers, instructed workers to defend "their" factories from attacks by "violent" students, and then sent letters to the press, in the name of the "workers' collective," congratulating the police for saving Yugoslav self-management from the violent students. "According to what is written and said, it turns out that it was the students who used force on the National Militia, that they blocked militia stations and surrounded them. Everything which has characterized the student movement from the beginning, in the city and in the university buildings, the order and self-control, is described with the old word: violence. . . This bureaucracy, which wants to create a conflict between workers and students, is inside the League of Communists, in the enterprises and in the state offices, and it is particularly powerful in the press (the press is an outstandingly hierarchic structure which leans on self-management only to protect itself from critiques and from responsibility). Facing the workers' and students' movement, the bureaucracy feels that it's losing the ground from under its feet, that it's losing those dark places where it prefers to move—and in fear cries out its meaningless claims. . . . Our movement urgently needs to tie itself with the working class. It has to explain its basic principles, and it has to ensure that these principles are realized, that they become richer and more complex, that they don't remain mere slogans. But this is precisely what the bureaucracy fears, and this is why they instruct workers to protect the factories from students, this is why they say that students are destroying the factories. What a monumental idiocy!" (D. Vuković in *Student*, June 8, 1968, p. 1.) Thus the self-managed directors of Yugoslav socialism protected Yugoslav workers from Yugoslav students just as, a few weeks earlier, the French "workers' organizations" (the

General Federation of Labor and the French Communist Party) had protected French workers from socialist revolution.

* * *

Repression and separation did not put an end to the Yugoslav revolutionary movement. General assemblies continued to take place, students continued to look for forms of organization which could unite them with workers, and which were adequate for the task of transforming society. The third step was to pacify and, if possible, to recuperate the movement so as to make it serve the needs of the very structure it had fought against. This step took the form of a major speech by Tito, printed in the June 11 issue of *Student*. In a society in which the vast majority of people consider the "cult of personality"in China the greatest sin on earth, the vast majority of students applauded the following words of the man whose picture has decorated all Yugoslav public institutions, many private houses, and most front pages of daily newspapers for a quarter of a century: ". . . Thinking about the demonstrations and what preceded them, I have reached the conclusion that the revolt of the young people, of the students, rose spontaneously. However, as the demonstrations developed and when later they were transfered from the street to university auditoriums, a certain infiltra—tion gradually took place on the part of foreign elements who wanted to use this situation for their own purposes. These include various tenden-cies and elements, from the most reactionary to the most extreme, seem-ingly radical elements who hold parts of Mao Tse Tung's theories." After this attempt to isolate and separate revolutionary students by shifting the problem from the content of the ideas to the source of the ideas (foreign elements with foreign ideas), the President of the Republic tries to recuperate the good, domestic students who only have local ideas. "However, I've come to the conclusion that the vast majority of students, I can say 90%, are honest youth. . . The newest develop-ments at the universities have shown that 90% of the students are our so-cialist youth, who do not let themselves be poisoned, who do not allow the various Djilasites, Rankovićites, Mao-Tse-Tungites realize their own goals on the pretext that they're concerned about the students. . . Our youth are good, but we have to devote more attention to them." Having told students how they should not allow themselves to be used, the President of Self-Managed Yugoslavia tells them how they should allow themselves to be used. "I turn, comrades and workers, to our students, so that they'll help us in a constructive approach and solution of all these prob-lems. May they follow what we're doing, that is their right; may they take part in our daily life, and when anything is not clear, when anything has to be cleared up, may they come to me. They can send a delegation." As for the content of the struggle, its goals, Tito speaks to kindergarten children and promises them that he will personally attend to every single one of their complaints. ". . . The revolt is partly a result of the fact that the students saw that I myself have often asked these questions, and even so they have remained unsolved. This time I promise students that I will engage myself on all sides to solve them, and in this students must help me. Furthermore, if I'm not able to solve these problems then I should no longer be on this place. I think that every old communist who has the consciousness of a communist should not insist on staying where he is, but should give his place to people who are able to solve problems. And finally I turn to students once again: it's time to return to your studies, it's time for tests, and I wish you success. It would really be a shame if you wasted still more time." (Tito in *Student*, June 11, 1968, pp. 1-2.)

This speech, which in itself represents a self-exposure, left open only two courses of action: either a further development of the movement completely outside of the clearly exposed political organizations, or else co-optation and temporary silence. The Yugoslav movement was co-opted and temporarily silenced. Six months after the explosion, in December, the Belgrade Student Union officially adopted the political action program proclaimed in June. This version of the program included a part I, on the social goals of the struggle, a Part II, on university reform, and a newly added Part III, on steps to be taken. In Part III it is explained that, "in realizing the program the method of work has to be kept in mind. 1) The Student Union is not able to participate directly in the solution of the general social problems (Part I of the program). . . 2) The Student Union is able to participate directly in the struggle to reform the University and the system of higher education as a whole (Part II of the program), and to be the spokesman of progressive trends in the University." (*Student*, December 17, 1969, p. 3.) Thus several events have taken place since June. The students' struggle has been institutionalized: it has been taken over by the "students' organization." Secondly, two new elements have been appended to the original goals of the June struggle: a program of university reform, and a method for realizing the goals. And finally, the initial goals of the struggle are abandoned to the social groups against whom the students had revolted. What was once an appendix has now become the only part of the program on which students are to act: "university reform." Thus the revolt against the managerial elite has been cynically turned into its opposite: the university is to be adapted to serve the needs of the dominant system of social relations; students are to be trained to serve the managerial elite more effectively.

While the "students' organization" initiates the "struggle" for university reform, the students, who had begun to organize themselves to struggle for very different goals, once again become passive and politically indifferent. "June was characterized by a birth of consciousness among the students; the period after June in many ways has the characteristics of the period before June, which can be explained by the inadequate reaction of society to the June events and to the goals expressed in June." (*Student*, May 13, 1969, p. 4.)

The struggle to overthrow the *status quo* has been turned away from its insanity; it has been made realistic; it has been transformed into a struggle to serve the *status quo*. This struggle, which the students do not engage in because "their organization" has assumed the task of managing it for them, is not accompanied by meetings, general assemblies or any other form of self-organization. This is because the students had not fought for "university reform" before June or during June, and they do not become recuperated for this "struggle" after June. It is in fact mainly the "students' spokesmen" who have become recuperated, because what was known before June is still known after June: "Improvement of the University makes sense only if it is based on the axiom that transformations of the university depend on transformations of the society. The present condition of the University reflects, to a greater or lesser extent, the condition of the society. In the light of this fact, it is meaningless to hold that we've argued about general social problems long enough, and that the time has come to turn our attention to university reform." (B. Jakšić in *Susret*, February 19, 1969.)

The content of "university reform" is defined by the Rector of the University of Belgrade. In his formulation, published in *Student* half a year after the June events, the Rector even includes "goals" which the students had specifically fought against, such as separation from the working class for a price, and the systematic integration of students, not only into the technocracy, but into the armed forces as well: "The struggle to improve the material position of the university and of students is our constant task. . . . One of the key questions of present-day work at the university is the imperative to struggle against all forms of defeatism and demagogy. Our university, and particularly our student youth, are and will be the enthusiastic and sure defense of our socialist homeland. Systematic organization in the building of the defensive power of our country against every aggressor, from whatever side he may try to attack us, must be the constant, quick and efficient work of all of us." (D. Ivanović in *Student*, October 15, 1968, p. 4.) These remarks were preceded by long and very abstract statements to the effect that "self-management is the content of university reform." The more specific remarks quoted above make it clear what the Rector understands to be the "content" of "self-management."

Since students do not eagerly throw themselves into the "struggle" for university reform, the task is left to the experts who are interested in it, the professors and the academic functionaries. "The main topics of conversation of a large number of teachers and their colleagues are automobiles, weekend houses and the easy life. These are also the main topics of conversation of the social elite which is so sharply criticized in the writings of these academics who do not grasp that they are an integral and not unimportant part of this elite." (B.Jakšić in *Susret*, February 19, 1969.)

Under the heading of University reform, one of Yugoslavia's leading (official) economists advocates a bureaucratic utopia with elements of magic. The same economist who, some years ago, had emphasized the arithmetical "balances of national production" developed by Soviet "social engineers" for application on human beings by a state bureaucracy, now advocates "the application of General Systems Theory for the analysis of concrete social systems." This General Systems Theory is the latest scientific discovery of "developed and progressive social systems"—like the United States. Due to this fact, "General Systems Theory has become indispensible for all future experts in fields of social science, and also for all other experts, whatever domain of social development they may participate in." (R. Stojanović, "On the Need to Study General Systems Theory at Social Science Faculties,"*Student*, February 25, 1969.) If, through university reform, General Systems Theory can be drilled into the heads of all future Yugoslav technocrats, presumably Yugoslavia will magically become a "developed and progressive social system"—namely a commercial, technocratic and military bureaucracy, a wonderland for human engineering.

* * *

The students have been separated from the workers; their struggle has been recuperated: it has become an occasion for academic bureaucrats to serve the commercial-technocratic elite more effectively. The bureaucrats encourage students to "self-manage" this "university reform," to participate in shaping themselves into businessmen, technicians and managers. Meanwhile, Yugoslav workers produce more than they've ever produced before, and watch the products of their labor increase the wealth and power of other social groups, groups which use that power against the workers. According to the Constitution, the workers govern themselves. However, according to a worker interviewed by *Student*, "That's only on paper. When the managers choose their people, workers have to obey; that's how it is here." (*Student*, March 4, 1969, p. 4.) If a worker wants to initiate a struggle against the continually increasing social inequality of wealth and power, he is checked by Yugoslavia's enormous unemployment: a vast reserve army of unemployed waits to replace him, because the only alternative is to leave Yugoslavia. The workers still have a powerful instrument with which to "govern themselves"; it is the same instrument workers have in capitalist societies: the strike. However, according to one analyst, strikes of workers who are separated from the revolutionary currents of the society and separated from the rest of the working class, namely "economic" strikes, have not increased the power of workers in Yugoslav society; the effect is nearly the opposite: "What has changed after eleven years of experience with strikes? Wherever they broke out, strikes reproduced precisely those relations which had led to strikes. For example, workers rebel because they're shortchanged in the distribution; then **someone**, probably the one who previously shortchanged them, gives them what he had taken from them; the strike ends and the workers continue to be hired laborers. And the one who gave in did so in order to maintain his position as the one who gives, the one who saves the workers. In other words, relations of wage-labor, which are in fact the main cause of the strike as a method for resolving conflicts, continue to be reproduced.   This leads to another question: is it at all possible for the working class to emancipate itself in a full sense within the context of an enterprise, or is that a process which has to develop on the level of the entire society, a process which does not tolerate any separation between different enterprises, branches, republics?" (*Susret*, April 18, 1969.)

As for the experts who shortchange the working class, *Student* carried a long description of various forms of expertise: "1) Enterprise functionaries (directors, businessmen, traveling salesmen, etc.) are paid by the managing board, the workers' council or other self-managed organs, for breaking legal statutes or moral norms in ways that are economically advantageous to the enterprise. . . 2). . . 3) Fictitious or simulated jobs are performed for purposes of tax evasion. . . 4). . . 5) Funds set aside for social consumption are given out for the cons--truction of private apartments, weekend houses, or for the purchase of automobiles. . ." (*Student*, February 18, 1969, p. 1.)

The official ideology of Socialist Yugoslavia does not conflict with the interests of its commercial-technocratic elite; in fact it provides a justification for those interests. In March, 1969, the Resolution of the Ninth Congress of the Yugoslav League of Communists referred to critiques by June revolutionaries only to reject them, and to reaffirm the official ideology. The absurd contention according to which commodity production remains the central social relation in "socialism" is restated in this document. "The economic laws of commodity production in socialism act as a powerful support to the development of modern productive forces and rational management." This statement is justified by means of the now-familiar demonology, namely by the argument that the only alternative to commodity production in "socialism" is Stalin: "Administrative-bureaucratic management of administration and social reproduction deforms real relations and forms monopolies, namely bureaucratic subjectivism in the conditions of management, and unavoidably leads to irrationality and parasitism in the distribution of the social product. . . "   Thus the choice is clear: either maintain the *status quo*, or else return to the system which the same League of Communists had imposed on Yugoslav society before 1948. The same type of demonology is used to demolish the idea that "to each according to his work," the official slogan of Yugoslavia, means what the words say. Such an interpretation "ignores differences in abilities and contributions. Such a demand leads to the formation of an all-powerful administrative, bureaucratic force, above production and above society; a force which institutes artificial and superficial equalization, and whose power leads to need, inequality and privilege. . . " (*Student*, March 18, 1969.) The principle "to each according to his work" was historically developed by the capitalist class in its struggle against the landed aristocracy, and in present day Yugoslavia this principle has the same meaning that it had for the bourgeoisie. Thus the enormous personal income (and bonuses) of a successful commercial entrepreneur in a Yugoslav import-export firm is justified with this slogan, since his financial success proves both his superior ability as well as the value of his contribution to society. In other words, distribution takes place in terms of the social evaluation of one's labor, and in a commodity economy labor is evaluated on the market. The result is a system of distribution which can be summarized by the slogan "from each according to his ability, to each according to his market success," a slogan which describes a system of social relations widely known as capitalist commodity production, and not as socialism (which was defined by Marx as the negation of capitalist commodity production).

The defense of this document was not characterized by more subtle methods of argument, but rather by the type of conservative complacency which simply takes the *status quo* for granted as the best of all possible worlds. "I can hardly accept critiques which are not consistent with the spirit of this material and with the basic ideas which it really contains. . . Insistence on a conception which would give rational solutions to all the relations and problems we confront, seems to me to go beyond the real possibilities of our society. . . This is our reality. The different conditions of work in individual enterprises, in individual branches, in individual regions of the country and elsewhere —we cannot eliminate them. . . " (V. Rakić in *Student*, March 11, 1969, p. 12.)

In another issue of *Student*, this type of posture was characterized in the following terms: "A subject who judges everything consistent and radical as an exaggeration identifies himself with what objectively exists; thus everything seems to him too idealistic, abstract, Quixotic, unreal, too far-fetched for our reality, and never for him. Numerous people, particularly those who could contribute to the transformation of society, continually lean on reality, on the obstacles which it presents, not seeing that often it is precisely they, with their superficial sense for reality, with their so-called *real-politik*, who are themselves the obstacles whose victims they claim to be." (D. Grlić in *Student*, April 28, 1969, p. 3.)

"We cannot allow ourselves to forget that democracy (not to speak of socialism) as well as self-government in an alienated and ideological form may become a dangerous instrument for promulgating and spreading the illusion that by 'introducing' it, namely through a proclamation, a decree on self-management, we've chosen the right to independent control, which *eo ipso* negates the need for any kind of struggle. Against whom, and why should we struggle when we already govern ourselves; now we are ourselves—and not anyone above us—guilty for all our shortcomings." (*Ibid.*)

The socialist ideology of Yugoslavia has been shown to be hollow; the ruling elite has been deprived of its justifications. But as yet the exposure has taken the form of critical analysis, of revolutionary theory. Revolutionary practice, self-organization by the base, as yet has little experience. In the meantime, those whose struggle for socialism has long ago become a struggle to keep themselves in power, continue to identify their own rule with self-government of the working class, they continue to define the commodity economy whose ideologues they have become as the world's most democratic society. In May 1969, the newly elected president of the Croatian parliament, long-time member of the Central Committee of the Yugoslav Communist Party, blandly stated that "the facts about the most basic indexes of our development show and prove that the economic development of the Socialist Republic of Croatia, and of Yugoslavia as a whole, has been harmonious and progressive." The president is aware of unemployment and the forced exile of Yugoslav workers, but the problem is about to be solved because "Some actions have been initiated to deal with the concern over our people who are temporarily employed abroad; these actions must be systematized, improved, and included as an integral part of our system, our economy and our polity. . . " The president is also aware of profound critiques of the present arrangement, and for him these are "illusions, confusions, desperation, impatience, Quixotic pretentions which are manifested—regardless of the seeming contradiction—from leftist revolutionary phrases to chauvinistic trends which take the form of philosophy, philology, movement of the labor force, economic situation of the nation, republic, etc. . . . We must energetically reject attempts to dramatize and generalize certain facts which, pulled out of the context of our entire development and our reality, attempt to use them for defeatist, demoralizing, and at times chauvinistic actions. We must systematically and factually inform our working people of these attempts, we must point out their elements, their methods, their real intentions, and the meaning of the actions." (J. Blažević, *Vjesnik*, May 9, 1969, p. 2.)

Official reactions to the birth of the Yugoslav "new left," from those of the President of Yugoslavia to those of the President of Croatia, are humorously summarized in a satire published on the front page of the May 13 issue of *Student.* ". . . Many of our opponents declare themselves for democracy, but what they want is some kind of pure or full democracy, some kind of libertarianism. In actual fact they're fighting for their own positions, so as to be able to speak and work according to their own will and the way they think right. We reject all the attempts of these anti-democratic forces; in our society it must be clear to everyone who is responsible to whom. . . In the struggle against these opponents, we're not going to use undemocratic means unless democratic means do not show adequate success. An excellent example of the application of democratic methods of struggle is our confrontation with bureaucratic forces. We all know that in the recent past, bureaucracy was our greatest social evil. And where is that bureaucracy now? It melted, like snow. Under the pressure of our self-managing mechanisms and our democratic forces, it melted all by itself, automatically, and we did not even need to make any changes whatever in the personnel or the structures of our national government, which in any case would not have been consistent with self-management. The opponents attack our large social differences, and they even call them unjustified. . . But the working class, the leading and ruling force of our society, the carrier of progressive trends and the historical subject, must not become privileged at the expense of other social categories; it must be ready to sacrifice in the name of the further construction of our system. The working class is aware of this and decisively rejects all demands for a radical decrease in social differences, since these are in essence demands for equalization; and this, above all else, would lead to a society of poor people. But our goal is a society in which everyone will be rich and will get according to his needs. . . The problem of unemployment is also constantly attacked by enemy forces. Opponents of our system argue that we should not make such a fuss about creating new jobs (as if that was as easy as opening windows in June), and that trained young people would accelerate the economic reform. . . In the current phase of our development we were not able to create more jobs, but we created another type of solution—we opened our frontiers and allowed our workers free employment abroad. Obviously it would be nice if we all had work here, at home. Even the Constitution says that. But that cannot be harmonized with the new phase of our reform. However, the struggle for reform has entered its final, conclusive stage and things will improve significantly. In actual fact, our people don't have it so bad even now. Earlier they could work only for one state, now they can work for the entire world. What's one state to the entire world? This creates mutual understanding and friendship. . . We were obviously unable to describe all the enemies of our system, such as various extremists, leftists, rightists, anarcho-liberals, radicals, demagogues, teachers, dogmatics, would-be-revolutionaries (who go so far as to claim that our revolution has fallen into crisis), anti-reformists and informal groups. . . , unitarians, folklorists, and many other elements. All of them represent potential hotbeds of crisis. All these informal groups and extremists must be energetically isolated from society, and if possible re-formed so as to prevent their destructive activity." (V. Teofilović in *Student*, May 13, 1969, p. 1.)

The Yugoslav experience adds new elements to the experience of the world revolutionary movement; the appearance of these elements

66

has made it clear that socialist revolution is not a historical fact in Yugoslavia's past, but a struggle in the future. This struggle has been initiated, but it has nowhere been carried out. "For as Babeuf wrote, managers organize a revolution in order to manage, but an authentic revolution is only possible from the bottom, as a mass movement. Society, all of its spontaneous human activity, rises as a historical subject and creates the identity of politics and popular will which is the basis for the elimination of politics as a form of human alienation." (M. Vojnović in *Student*, April 22, 1969, p. 1.) Revolution in this sense cannot even be conceived within the confines of a single university, a single factory, a single nation-state. Furthermore, revolution is not the repetition of an event which already took place, somewhere, sometime; it is not the reproduction of past relations, but the creation of new ones. In the words of another Yugoslav writer, "it is not only a conflict between **production** and **creation**, but in a larger sense—and here I have in mind the West as well as the East—between **routine** and **adventure**." (M. Krleža in *Politika*, December 29, 1968; quoted in *Student*, January 7, 1969.)

1969

Ten Theses on the Proliferation of Egocrats

I

The Egocrat - Mao, Stalin, Hitler, Kim, Il Sung - is not an accident or an aberration or an irruption of irrationality; he is a personification of the relations of the existing social order.

II

The Egocrat is initially an individual, like everyone else: mute and powerless in this society without community or communication, victimized by the spectacle, "the existing order's uninterrupted discourse about itself, its laudatory monologue, the self-portrait of power in the epoch of its totalitarian management of the conditions of existence." (Debord) Repelled by the spectacle, he longs for "the liberated human being, a being who is at once a social being and a *Gemeinwesen*." (Camatte) If his longing were expressed in practice: at his workplace, in the street, wherever the spectacle robs him of his humanity, he would become a rebel.

III

The Egocrat does not express his longing for community and communication in practice; he transforms it into a Thought. Armed with this Thought, he is still mute and powerless, but is no longer like everyone else: he is Conscious, he possesses the Idea. To confirm his difference, to make sure he's not deluding himself, he needs to be seen as different by others - those others who confirm that he is truly a possessor of the Thought and a possessor of the True Thought.

IV

The Egocrat finds "community" and "communication," not by smashing the elements of the spectacle in his reach, but by surrounding himself with like-minded individuals, other Egos, who reflect the Golden Thought to each other and confirm each other's validity as possessors of It. Chosen People. At this point the Thought, if it is to remain golden, must evermore remain the same: unsullied and uncompromised; criticism and revision are synonyms of betrayal. "Thus it can only exist as a polemic with reality. It refutes everything. It can survive only by freezing, by becoming increasingly totalitarian." (Camatte) Therefore, in order to continue to reflect and confirm the Thought, the individual must stop thinking.

V

The initial goal, the "liberated human being," is lost to practice when it is relegated to the Egocrat's consciousness, because "consciousness makes itself the goal and reifies itself in an organization which comes to incarnate the goal." (Camatte) The group of mutual admirers acquires a schedule and a meeting place; it becomes an institution. The organization, which takes the form of a Bolshevik or Nazi cell, a Socialist reading club, or an Anarchist affinity group, depending on local circumstances and individual preferences, "provides a terrain favorable to informal domination by propagandists and defenders of their ideology, specialists who are in general more mediocre the more their intellectual activity consists of the repetition of certain definitive truths. Ideological respect for unanimity of decision has on the whole been favorable to the uncontrolled authority, within the organization itself, of *specialists in freedom*" (wrote Debord, describing anarchist organizations). Rejecting the ruling spectacle ideologically, the organization of specialists in freedom reproduces the relation of the spectacle in its internal practice.

VI

The organization incarnating the Thought turns on the world, because "the project of this consciousness is to frame reality with its concept." (Camatte) The group becomes militant. It sets out to extend to society at large the organization's internal relations, one variant of which can be summarized as follows: "Within the party, there must be no one lagging behind when an order is given by th leadership to 'march forward,' no one turning right when the order is 'left.' " (- a revolutionary leader, quoted by M. Velli.) At this point the specific content of the Thought is as irrelevant to practice as the geography of the Christian paradise, because the goal is reduced to a cudgel: it serves as the justification for the group's repressive practices, and as an instrument of blackmail. (Examples: "To deviate from socialist ideology in the slightest degree means strengthening bourgeois ideology" (- Lenin, quoted by M. Velli; "When 'libertarians' slanderously trash others, I question their maturity and commitment to revolutionary social change" an 'anarchist'

69

in a letter to *The Fifth Estate*.)

VII

The militant organization extends itself by means of conversion and manipulation. Conversion is the favored technique of early Bolshevism and missionary anarchism: the militant's explicit task is to introduce consciousness into the working class (Lenin), to "reach working people with our ideas" (an "anarchist" in "The Red Menace," Toronto). But the militant's implicit task, and the practical outcome of his activity, is to affect the practice of the workers, not their thought. The conversion is successful if workers, whatever their ideas, pay dues to the organization and obey the organization's calls to action (strikes, demonstrations, etc.) The Egocrat's implicit aim is to establish h s (and his organization's) hegemony over a large number of individuals, to become the leader of a mass of followers. This implicit aim becomes cynically explicit when the militants are Nazis or Stalinists (or an amalgam of the two, such as the US Labor Party). Conversion gives way to manipulation, outright lying. In this model, the recruitment of followers is the explicit aim, and the Idea ceases to be a fixed star, perfect and immutable; the Idea becomes a mere means toward the explicit aim; whatever recruits most followers is a good Idea; the Idea becomes a cynically constructed collage based on the fears and hatreds of potential followers; its main promise is the annihilation of scapegoats: "counter-revolutionaries," "anarchists," "CIA agents," "Jews," etc. The difference between manipulators and missionaries is theoretical; in practice, they are contemporaries competing in the same social field, and they borrow each other's techniques.

VIII

In order to broadcast the Idea, so as to convert or manipulate, the Egocrat needs instruments, media, and it is precisely such media that the society of the spectacle provides in profusion. One justification for turning to these media runs as follows: "The media are currently a monopoly of the ruling classes who *divert* them for their own benefit. But their *structure* remains 'fundamentally egalitarian,' and it is up to revolutionary practice to bring out this potentiality contained by them but perverted by the capitalist order in a word, to liberate them..." (a position paraphrased by Baudrillard.) The initial rejection of the spectacle, the longing for community and communication, has been replaced by the longing to exert power over the very instruments that annihilate community and communication. Hesitation, or a sudden outburst of critique, are ruled out by organizational blackmail: "The Leninists will win unless we ourselves accept the responsibility of fighting to win...," ("The Red Menace." A Stalinist would say, "The Trotskyists will win....," etc.) From this point on, anything goes; all means are good if they lead to the goal; and at the absurd outer limit, even sales promotion and advertising, the activity and language of Capital itself, become justified revolutionary means: "We concentrate heavily on distribution and promotion...Our promotional work is wide-ranging and expensive. It includes advertising widely, promotional m ailings, catalogues, display tables across the country, etc. All of this costs a tremendous amount of money and energy, which is covered by the money generated from the sale of books." (- An "anarchist businessman" in a letter to *The Fifth Estate*.) Is this anarchist businessman a ludicrous example, because so ridiculously exaggerated, or is he solidly within the orthodox tradition of organized militancy? "The big banks are the 'state apparatus' which we need to bring about socialism, and which we take ready made from capitalism; our task here is merely to lop off what capitalistically mutilates this excellent apparatus, to make it EVEN BIGGER, even more democratic, even more comprehensive..." (Lenin, quoted by M. Velli.)

IX

For the Egocrat, the media are mere means; the goal is hegemony, power the power of the secret police. "Invisible pilots in the center of the popular storm, we must direct it, not with a visible power, but with the collective dictatorship of all the allies. A dictatorship without a badge, without title, without official right, yet all the more powerful because it will have none of the appearances of power." (Bakunin, quoted by Debord) The collective dictatorship of all quickly becomes the rule of the single Egocrat because, "if all the bureaucrats taken together decide everything, the cohesion of their own class can be assured only by the concentration of their terrorist power in a single person." (Debord) With the success of the Egocrat's enterprise, the establishment of the "dictatorship without official right," communication is not only absent on a social scale; every local attempt is deliberately liquidated by the police. This situation is not a "deformation" of the organization's initially "pure goals"; it is already prefigured in the means, the "fundamentally egalitarian" instruments used for the victory . "What characterizes the mass media is the fact that they are anti-mediators, intransitives, the fact that they produce non-communication... Television, by its presence alone, is social control in the home. It is not necessary to imagine this control as the regime's periscope spying on the private life of everyone, because

71

television is already better than that: it assures that *people no longer talk to each other*, that they are definitively isolated in the face of statements without response." (Baudrillard)

X

The Egocrat's project is superfluous. The capitalist media of production and communication already reduce human beings to mute and powerless spectators, passive victims continually subjected to the existing order's "laudatory monologue." The anti-totalitarian revolution requires, not another medium, but the liquidation of all media, "the liquidation of their entire present structure, functional as well as technical, of their operational form so to speak, which everywhere reflects their social form. At the limit, obviously, it is the very concept of medium which disappears and must disappear: the exchanged word, reciprocal and symbolic exchange, negates the notion and function of medium, of intermediary... Reciprocity comes about by way of the destruction of the medium." (Baudrillard)

1977

References: Jean Baudrillard, *Pour une critique de l'economie politique du signe* (Paris, Gallimard, 1972), Jacques Camatte, *The Wandering of Humanity* (Detroit, Black & Red, 1975), Guy Debord, *Society of the Spectacle* (Detroit, Black & Red, 1970; 1977), Claude Lefort, *Un Homme en Trop: Reflexions sur "L'Archipel de Goulag,"* (Paris, Seuil, 1976), Michael Velli, *Manual for Revolutionary Leaders* (Detroit, Black & Red, 1972).

The Destruction of the Continent and Its Peoples

Progress & Nuclear Power

The premeditated poisoning of human beings, of soils and of other living species can only by the grossest hypocrisy be considered an "accident." Only the wilfully blind can claim that this consequence of Technical Progress was "unforeseen."

The poisoning and removal of this continent's living inhabitants for the sake of "higher entities" may have begun in Eastern Pennsylvania, but not during the past few weeks.

Eleven score years ago, in the region currently being poisoned by radiation from Three Mile Island, speculators with names like Franklin, Morris, Washington and Hale hid their names behind facades such as the Vandalia Company and the Ohio Company. These companies had one purpose: to sell land for a profit. The individuals behind the companies had one aim: to remove all obstacles which stood in the way of the free deployment of profit-making, whether the obstacles were human beings or millennial cultures or forests or animals or even streams and mountains. Their aim was to Civilize this continent, to introduce to it a cycle of activities never before practiced here: Working, Saving, Investing, Selling - the cycle of reproducing and enlarging Capital.

The main obstacle to this activity consisted of human beings who had lived on this continent for millennia and who, without Law or Government or Church, enjoyed the sun, the streams, the woodlands, the varied species of plant and animal, and each other. These people considered life an end, not a means to be put at the service of "higher" ends. They did not flock to Civilization like children to a cookie jar, as the Franklins and Washingtons expected them to do. On the contrary. They wanted very little of what Civilization had to give. They wanted some of the weapons, and they wanted these only to preserve their freedom against further encroachments of Civilization; they preferred death to a life reduced to Working, Saving, Investing and Selling. In a final desperate attempt to drive Civilization and its Benefits to the sea and across it, in an uprising currently remembered as the name of an automobile, their warriors ousted land grabbers and their soldiers from Ontario, Michigan, Ohio and western Pennsylvania. For this uncompromising resistance they earned from the Civilized the title of Savages. This title gave the Civilizers a licence to exterminate without qualm or scruple: "Send them pox-infested blankets," ordered one of the commanders in charge of the extermination.

The recently celebrated Bicentennial of American Independence commemorated the day when, tenscore years ago, land grabbers, speculators and their allies determined to accelerate the extermination of independence from the region west of Three Mile Island. The King's government was too distant to protect investments adequately, and in any case it was Feudal and didn't always share the speculators' aims; it even went so far as to enforce the boundaries established by treaties with the Savages. What was needed was an efficient apparatus under the direct control of the land grabbers and devoted exclusively to the prosperity of their enterprises. Informal frontier police organizations like the Paxton Boys were efficient for the massacre of the tribal inhabitants of an isolated village like Conestoga. But such frontier formations were small and temporary, and they were as dependent on the active consent of each participant as the tribal warriors themselves; therefore they were not proper police organizations at all. The speculators allied themselves with idealists and dreamers, and behind a banner on which was inscribed Freedom, Independence and Happiness, took the power of government, military and police into their own hands.

One and half centuries ago, the efficient apparatus for the progress of Capital was in high gear. Military and police organizations based on obedience and submission, and not on anyone's active consent, were ready to go into action against people who had resisted that type of regimentation for twenty thousand years if not longer. Congress passed one of its most explicit bits of legislation: The Indian Removal Act. Within a few years, all resistance, all activity which was not the activity of Capital, was removed from the area stretching westward from Three Mile Island to the Mississippi, southward from Michigan to Georgia. The Government, quickly becoming one of the most powerful in the world, was no longer restricted to poisoning with pox or to the surprise massacre of villagers; it implemented the Removal with a judicious combination of Platitudes, Promises and Police. The remaining free tribespeople could not resist this combination without adopting it, but they could not adopt it without ceasing to be free. They chose to remain free, and the last free human beings between Three Mile Island and the Mississippi were Removed.

As settlers moved into the deliberately vacated lands where the very air they breathed gave them a taste of the recently eliminated freedom, they transformed vast woodlands into enlarged replicas of the hell they had left behind. The enjoyment of trails and forests ceased: the forests were burned; the trails became obstacle courses to be traversed as rapidly as Capital made possible. Joy ceased to be life's aim; life itself became a mere means; its end was profit. The variety of hundreds of cultural forms was reduced to the uniformity of a unique routine: work, save, invest, sell, every day from sunrise to sunset, and count money after sundown. Every previous activity, and scores of new ones, were transformed from sources of joy to sources of profit. Corn, beans and squash, the "three sisters" respected and loved by the region's previous inhabitants, became mere commodities for sale at food markets; their sowers and harvesters no longer grew them to enjoy at meals, feasts and festivals, but to sell for a profit. Leisurely gardening was replaced by the hard work of farming, trails gave way to rails, walking was superseded by the locomotion of gigantic coal-burning furnaces on wheels, canoes were swept aside by floating cities which stopped for no obstacle as they filled the air with burning embers and black smoke. The "three sisters," along with the rest of their family, were degraded to mere merchandise, as were the trees that became lumber, the animals that became meat, and even the journeys, the songs, the myths and tales of the continent's new inhabitants.

And new inhabitants there were: at first hundreds, then thousands, finally millions. When the importation of outright slaves finally ended, surplus peasants were imported from the run-down estates of post-feudal Europe. Their ancestors hadn't known freedom for so many generations that the very memory of it had been lost. Formerly liveried domestics or farmhands on the estates of increasingly commercial lords, the newcomers arrived already trained to want precisely what Capital had to offer, and the degradation of life imposed by Capital was freedom to them when compared to their only frame of reference. Sold plots by land investors, transported to the plots by railway investors, equipped by farm implement investors, financed by bank investors, furnished and clothed by the same interests, often by the very same Houses who had provided them with everything else at a rate of profit no previous age would have regarded as "just," they boastfully wrote their relatives in the old country that they had become their own lords, that they were free farmers but in the pits of their stomachs and in the missed beat of their hearts they felt the truth: they were slaves of a master who was even more intractable, inhuman and removed than their former lords, a master whose lethal power, like radioactivity's, could be felt but not seen. They had become the liveried domestics of Capital. (As for those who ended up as "operatives" or "unskilled hands" in the factories that produced the implements and the rails: they had little to boast of in their letters; they had breathed freer air wherever they had started from.)

A century after the uprising associated with the name of Pontiac, a century filled with desperate resistance by Pontiac's successors against the further encroachments of Capital, some of the imported farmers began to fight against their reduction to servants of railroad, equipment and finance Capital. The populist farmers burned to arrest and lock up the Rockefellers, Morgans and Goulds directly responsible for their degradation, but their revolt was only a faint echo of the earlier revolt of Ottowas, Chippewas, Delawares and Potawatomies. The farmers turned against the personalities but continued to share the culture responsible for their degradation. Consequently they failed to unite with, or even recognize as their own, the armed resistance of the plains people, the last attempt to keep the entire continent from being turned into an island of Capital - a struggle defeated by ancient Assyrian (and modern Soviet Socialist) methods of mass deportation, concentration camps, massacres of unarmed prisoners, and unabated brainwashing by military and missionary goons.

Militant and courageous though many of them were, the struggling farmers rarely placed enjoyment and life above work, savings and profit, and their movement was derailed altogether when radical politicians infiltrated it and equated the desire for a new life with the desire for a new Leader. The form of derailment of the Populist movement became the form of existence of the Labor movement during the century that followed. The politicians who dug the grave of populism were the forerunners of the infinite assortment of monkish sects, modelled organizationally on the Jesuit Order but deriving doctrine and dogma from one or another communist, socialist or anarchist Book. Ready to leap at an instant's notice into any situation where people began to struggle to regain their own humanity, they squelched one after another potential rebellion by dumping their doctrine, their organization and their leadership on top of people struggling for life. These clowns, for whom all that was missing was their mugs and speeches on the front pages of newspapers, finally became capitalists who took to market the unique commodity they had cornered: Labor.

Shortly before the turn of the present century, with effective resistance permanently removed, with a pseudo-resistance which was in fact an instrument for the final reduction of human activity to a mere variable of Capital, the efficient apparatus for the generation of profits lost all external obstacles. It still had internal obstacles: the various fractions of Capital, the Vanderbilts, Goulds and Morgans, continually turned their guns against each other and threatened to topple the whole structure from within. Rockefeller and Morgan pioneered the merger, the combination of the various fractions: monied investors distributed their monies throughout each other's enterprises; directors sat on each other's boards; and each and all acquired an interest in the unrestricted march of every unit of the entire apparatus. With the exception of rare surviving personal and family empires, the enterprises were directed by mere hirelings who differed from the rest of the hands mainly by the size of their emoluments. The task of the directors was to ride over all obstacles, human and natural, with only one limitation: the efficient operation of the other enterprises collectively constituting Capital.

Twoscore years ago, the researches of physical and chemical sciences at the disposal of Capital led to the discovery that the gross substances above and below the soil were not the only substances exploitable for profits. It appeared that the "liberated" nuclei of certain substances were eminently exploitable by Capital. The destruction of matter at the atomic level, first used as the most hideous weapon hitherto wrought by human beings, became the newest commodity. By this time the interest payments, freight fees and equipment purchases of farmers, as well as the long-vanished trees and forest animals, had ceased to be interesting as sources of significant profits. Energy companies interlocked with uranium and oil monopolies became empires more powerful than any of the states which served them as trouble-shooters. Within the computers of these empires, the health and lives of an "acceptable" number of farm and city dwellers was balanced against an "acceptable" gain or loss of profits. Potential popular responses to such calculations were controlled by judicious combinations of platitudes, promises and police.

* * *

* The poisoning of people in Eastern Pennsylvania with cancer-inducing radiation by a system that devotes a substantial portion of its activity to "defense" against nuclear assault from abroad-

* The contamination of food which is to be consumed by the continent's remaining inhabitants, and the destruction of the prospects of farmers who had dutifully devoted their lives to growing the merchandise interesting to Capital at a stage which ended half a century ago-

* The transformation into a literal minefield, using unprecedentedly lethal poisons and explosives, of a continent once peopled by human beings whose aim in life was to enjoy the air, sun, trees, animals and each other-

* The prospect of a continent covered with raging infernos, their loud-speakers reciting their recorded messages to a charred earth: "There is no need to overreact; the situation is stable; the leaders have everything under control"-

-all this is no accident. It is the present stage of progress of Technology, alias Capital, called Frankenstein by Mary Wollstonecraft Shelley, considered "neutral" by aspiring managers burning to get their "revolutionary" hands on the controls. For two hundred years Capital developed by destroying nature, by removing and destroying human beings. Capital has now begun a frontal attack on its own domestics; its computers have begun to calculate the expendability of those who'd been taught to think themselves its beneficiaries.

If the spirits of the dead could be reborn among the living. Ottawa and Chippewa and Potawatomi warriors could take up the struggle where they left it two centuries ago, augmented by the forces of Sioux, Dakota and Nez Percé, Yana and Medoc and the countless tribes whose languages are no longer spoken. Such a force could round up criminals who would not otherwise be brought before any tribunal. The numerous agents of Capital could then continue to practice their routine of work-save-invest-sell, torturing each other with platitudes, promises and police, inside defused and disconnected power plants behind plutonium doors.

1979

Anti-Semitism and the Beirut Pogrom

Escape from death in a gas chamber or a Pogrom, or incarceration in a concentration camp, may give a thoughtful and capable writer, Solzhenitsyn for example, profound insights into many of the central elements of contemporary existence, but such an experience does not, in itself, make Solzhenitsyn a thinker, a writer, or even a critic of concentration camps; it does not, in itself, confer any special powers. In another person the experience might lie dormant as a potentiality, or remain forever meaningless, or it might contribute to making the person an ogre. In short, the experience is an indelible part of the individual's past but it does not determine his future; the individual is free to choose his future; he is even free to choose to abolish his freedom, in which case he chooses in bad faith and is a *Salaud* (J.P. Sartre's precise philosophical term for a person who makes such a choice).*

My observations are borrowed from Sartre; I'd like to apply them, not to Solzhenitsyn, but to myself, as a specific individual, and to the American cheerleaders rooting for the State of Israel, as a specific choice.

* * *

I was one of three small children removed by our elders from a Central European country a month before the Nazis invaded the country and began rounding up Jews. Only part of my extended family left; the rest remained and were all rounded up; of these, all my cousins, aunts, and grandparents died in Nazi concentration camps or gas chambers except two uncles, whom I'll mention later.

A month more and I, too, would have been one of those who actually underwent the rationally-planned scientific extermination of human beings, the central experience of so many people in an age of highly developed science and productive forces, but I wouldn't have been able to write about it.

I was one of those who escaped. I spent my childhood

*The usual English translation is "Bastard."

among Quechua-speaking people of the Andean highlands, but I didn't learn to speak Quechua and I didn't ask myself why; I spoke to a Quechua in a language foreign to both of us, the Conquistador's language. I wasn't aware of myself as a refugee nor of the Quechuas as refugees in their own land; I knew no more about the terrors—the expropriations, persecutions and progroms, the annihilation of an ancient culture—experienced by their ancestors than I knew about the terrors experienced by mine.

To me the Quechuas were generous, hospitable, guileless, and I thought more of an aunt who respected and liked them than of a relative who cheated them and was contemptuous of them and called them dirty and primitive.

My relative's cheating was my first contact with the double standard, the fleecing of outsiders to enrich insiders, the moral adage that said: It's all right if it's We who do it.

My relative's contempt was my first experience with racism, which gave this relative an affinity with the Pogromists she had fled from; her narrow escape from them did not make her a critic of Pogromists; the experience probably contributed nothing to her personality, not even her identification with the Conquistador, since this was shared by Europeans who did not share my relative's experience of narrowly escaping from a concentration camp. Oppressed European peasants had identified with Conquistadores who carried a more vicious oppression to non-Europeans already before my relative's experience.

My relative did make use of her experience years later, when she chose to be a rooter for the State of Israel, at which time she did not renounce her contempt toward the Quechuas; on the contrary, she then applied her contempt toward people in other parts of the world, people she had never met or been among. But I wasn't concerned with the character of her choice at the time; I was more concerned with the chocolates she brought me.

* * *

In my teens I was brought to America, which was a synonym for New York even to people already in America among the Quechuas; it was a synonym for much else, as I was very slowly to learn.

Shortly after my arrival in America, the state power of the Central European country of my origin was seized by a well-organized gang of egalitarians who thought they could bring about universal emancipation by occupying State offices and becoming policemen, and the new State of Israel fought its first successful war and turned an indigenous population of Semites into internal refugees like the Quechuas and exiled refugees like the Central European Jews. I should have wondered why the Semitic refugees and the European refugees who claimed to be Semitic, two peoples with so much in common, did not make common cause against common oppressors, but I was far too occupied trying to find my way in America.

From an elementary school friend who was considered a hooligan by my parents, and also from my parents themselves, I slowly learned that America was the place where anyone would want to be, something like Paradise, but a Paradise that remained out of reach even after one entered America. America was a land of clerks and factory workers, but neither clerical nor factory work were America. My hooligan friend summarized it all very simply: there were suckers and hustlers, and you had to be dumb to become a sucker. My parents were less explicit; they said: Study hard. The implied motivation was: God forbid you should become a clerk or factory worker! Become something other: a professional or a manager. At that time I didn't know these other callings were also America's, that with every rung reached, Paradise remained as unreachable as before. I didn't know that the professional's or even the clerk's or worker's satisfaction came, not from the fullness of his own life, but from the rejection of his own life, from identification with the great process taking place outside him, the process of unfettered industrial destruction. The results of this process could be watched in movies or newspapers, though not yet on Television, which would soon bring the process into everyone's home; the satisfaction was that of the voyeur, the peeper. At that time I didn't know that this process was the most concrete synonym for America.

Once in America, I had no use for my experience of narrowly escaping a Nazi concentration camp; the experience couldn't help me climb the ladder toward Paradise and might even hinder me; my hurried climb might have been slowed considerably or even stopped altogether if I had tried to empathize with the condition of the labor camp inmate I might have become, for I would have realized what it was that made the prospect of factory work so fearsome: it differed from the other condition in that there were no gas chambers and in that the factory worker spent only his weekdays inside.

I wasn't alone in having no use for my Central European experience. My relatives had no use for it either. During that decade I met one of my two uncles who had actually lived through a Nazi concentration camp. Once in America, even this uncle had no use for his experience; he wanted nothing more than to forget the Pogrom and everything associated with it; he wanted only to climb the rungs of America; he wanted to look and sound and act no differently from other Americans. My parents had exactly the same attitude. I was told that my other uncle had survived the camps and gone to Israel, only to be hit by a car soon after his arrival.

The State of Israel was not interesting to me during that decade, although I heard talk of it. My relatives spoke with a certain pride of the existence of a State with Jewish policemen, a Jewish army, Jewish judges and factory managers, in short a State totally unlike Nazi Germany and just like America. My relatives, whatever their personal situations, identified with the Jewish policemen and not with the policed, with the factory owners and not the Jewish workers, with the Jewish hustlers and not the suckers, an identification which was understandable among people who wanted to forget their close encounter with labor camps. But none of them wanted to go there; they were already in America.

My relatives gave grudgingly to the Zionist cause and were baffled—all except my racist relative—by the unqualified enthusiasm of second to n^{th} generation Americans for a distant State with Jewish policemen and teachers and managers, since these people were already policemen and teachers and managers in America. My racist relative understood what the enthusiasm was based on: racial solidarity. But I wasn't aware of this at the time. I was not an overbright American high-schooler and I thought racial solidarity was something confined to Nazis, Afrikaaners and American Southerners.

I was starting to be familiar with the traits of the Nazis who'd almost captured me: the racism that reduced human beings to their genealogical connections over five or six generations, the crusading nationalism that considered the rest of humanity an obstacle, the *Gleichschaltung* that cut off the individual's freedom to choose, the technological efficiency that made small humans mere fodder for great machines, the bully militarism that pitted walls of tanks against a cavalry and exacted a hundred times the losses it sustained, the official paranoia that pictured the enemy, poorly armed townspeople and villagers, as a nearly omnipotent conspiracy of cosmic scope. But I didn't see that these traits had anything to do with America or Israel.

* * *

It was only during my next decade, as an American college student with a mild interest in history and philosophy, that I began to acquire a smattering of knowledge about Israel and Zionism, not because I was particularly interested in these subjects but because they were included in my readings. I was neither hostile nor friendly; I was indifferent; I still had no use for my experience as a refugee.

But I didn't remain indifferent to Israel or Zionism. This was the decade of Israel's spectacular capture and trial of the Good German Eichmann, and of Israel's spectacular invasion of large parts of Egypt, Syria and Jordan in a six-day *Blitzkrieg,* a decade when Israel was news for everyone, not just for refugees.

I didn't have any unconventional thoughts about the obedient Eichmann except the thought that he couldn't be so exceptional, since I had already met people like him in America. But some of my readings did make me start wondering about my Zionist relative's racism.

I learned that people like the ancient Hebrews, Akkadians, Arabs, Phoenicians and Ethiopians had all come from the land of Shem (the Arabian Peninsula) and had all spoken the language of Shem, which was what made them Shemites or Semites. I learned that the Jewish religion had originated among Semites in the ancient Levantine State Judah, the Christian religion among Semites in the ancient Levantine towns Nazareth and Jerusalem, the Mohammedan religion among Semites in the ancient Arabian towns Mecca and Medina, and that for the past 1300 years the region called Palestine had been a sacred place to the Islamic Semites who lived there and in surrounding regions.

I also learned that the religions of European and American Jews, like the religions of European and American Christians, had been elaborated, during almost two millennia, by Europeans and more recently by Americans.

If Europeans and American Jews were Semites in terms of their religion, then European and American Christians were also Semites, a notion that was generally considered absurd.

If Jews were Semites in terms of the language of their Sacred Book, then all European and American Christians were Greeks or Italians, a notion almost as patently absurd.

I started to suspect that my Zionist relative's only connection to the Zion in the Levant was a genealogical connection traced, not over six, but over more than sixty generations. But I had come to consider such racial reckoning a peculiarity of Nazis, Afrikaaners and American Southerners.

I was uneasy. I thought surely there was more to it than that; surely those who claimed to descend from the victims of all that racism were not carriers of a racism ten times more thorough.

I knew little of the Zionist Movement, but enough to start being repelled. I knew the Movement had originally had two wings, one of which, the Socialist one, I could understand because I was starting to empathize with victims of oppression, not from insights I gained from my own experience but from books equally accessible to others; the other wing of Zionism was incomprehensible to me.

The egalitarian or Left Zionists, as I then understood them, did not want to be assimilated into the European states that persecuted them, some because they didn't think they ever could be, others because they were repelled by industrializing Europe and America. The Messiah, their Movement, would deliver Israel from exile and guide her to Zion, to something altogether different, to a Paradise without suckers or hustlers. Some of them, even more metaphorically, hoped the Messiah would deliver the oppressed from their oppressors, if not everywhere, then at least in a millennial egalitarian Utopia located in a province of the Ottoman Empire, and they were ready to join with the Islamic residents of Zion against Ottoman, Levantine and British oppressors. They shared this dream with Christian millenarians who had been trying for more than a millennium to found Zion in one or another province of Europe; both had the same roots, but I suspected the left Zionists had inherited their millenarianism from the Christians.

The egalitarian Zionists were arrogant in thinking the Islamic residents of Zion would embrace European leftists as liberators, and they were as naive as the egalitarians who had seized state power in the country of my birth, thinking the millennium would begin as soon as they occupied State offices and became policemen. But as far as I could see, they weren't racists.

The other Zionists, the Right, who by the time I reached college had all but supplanted the Left, at least in America, were explicit racists and assimilationists; they wanted a State dominated by a Race ever so thinly disguised as a religion, a State that would not be something altogether different, but exactly the same as America and the other states in the Family of Nations. I couldn't understand this, for it seemed to me that these Zionists, who included statists, industrializers and technocrats, were not only racists but also Conversos.

Earlier Conversos were Jews in fifteenth century Spain who, to avoid persecution, discovered that the long-awaited Jewish Messiah had already arrived, a millennium and a half earlier, in the person of Jewish prophet Jesse, the Crucified. Some of these Conversos then joined the Inquisition and persecuted Jews who had not made this discovery.

The modern Conversos hadn't become Catholics; Catholicism was not the dominant creed in the twentieth century; Science and Technology were.

I thought Jesse had at least affirmed, if only as relics, some of the traits of the ancient human community, whereas Science and Technology affirmed nothing human; they destroyed culture as well as nature as well as human community.

It seemed sad that the long-preserved and carefully-guarded specificities of a cultural minority that had refused to be absorbed were to shatter on the discovery that the technocratic State was the Messiah and the Industrial Process the long-awaited millennium. This made the whole trajectory meaningless. The dream of these racist Conversos was repulsive to me.

* * *

It wasn't until the following decade, when I was over thirty, that my nearness to the Nazi Pogrom began to be meaningful to me. This transvaluation of my early experience happened suddenly, and was caused by something like a chance encounter, an encounter which, also by chance, included an odd reference to the State of Israel.

This was the decade when America waged its war of extermination against a people and an ancient culture of the Far East.

It happened that I was visiting my Americanized relatives at the same time that my Andean aunt was with them for the first time since their separation. This was the aunt who had respected the Quechua-speaking people, although not enough to learn their language, and had stayed among them when the others left.

The conversation among the relatives turned to pious reflections about the uncle who had gone to Israel and been killed by a car after having survived the Nazi concentration camps.

My Andean aunt couldn't believe what she heard. She asked her relatives if they had all gone crazy. The story about the car accident had been told to the children so often that the adults had come to believe it.

That man wasn't killed in an accident, she shouted. He committed suicide. He had survived the concentration camps because he had been a technician employed in applying chemical science to the operation of the gas chambers. He had then made the mistake of emigrating to Israel, where his collaboration had been made public knowledge. He probably couldn't face the accusing eyes; maybe he feared retaliation.

My first response to this revelation was revulsion against a human being who could be so morally degraded as to gas his own kin and fellow-captives. But the more I thought about him, the more I had to admit there had at least been a shred of moral integrity in his final self-destructive act; that act didn't make him a moral paradigm, but it contrasted sharply with the acts of people who lacked even that shred of moral integrity, people who were returning from the Far East and affirming their deeds, actually boasting of the unnatural atrocities they had inflicted on their fellow human beings.

And I asked myself who the others really were, the pure ones who had exposed and judged Eichmann the obedient German.

I didn't know anything about the people in Israel and had never met an Israeli, but I was increasingly aware of the loud American cheerleaders for the State of Israel, and not the Left Zionists among them but the others, my racist relative's friends. The Leftists had all but vanished in a dark sectarian Limbo no outsider could penetrate, a Limbo that stank almost as strongly as the one that held Messiah Lenin's and Stalin's heirs, with sects twisted out of shape by the existence of the State of Israel, ranging from those who claimed their seizure of power was all that was needed to turn the State of Israel into an egalitarian community, to those who claimed the existing State of Israel was already the egalitarian community.

But the Left Zionists shouted only at each other.

It was the others who made all the din, who shouted at everyone else. And these were explicit about what they admired in the State of Israel; they affirmed it, they boasted of it, and it had nothing to do with the ailing wing's egalitarianism. What they admired was:

—the crusading nationalism that considered the humanity surrounding it as nothing but obstacles to its flowering;

—the industrial potency of the Race that had succeeded in denaturing the desert and making it bloom;

—the efficiency of the human beings remade into operators of big tanks and incredibly accurate jets;

—the technological sophistication of the instruments of death themselves, infinitely superior to that of the Nazis;

—the spectacularly enterprising secret police whose prowess was surely not inferior, for such a small State, to that of the CIA, KGB or Gestapo;

—the bully militarism that pitted the latest inventions of life-killing Science against a motley collection of weapons, and exacted a hundred or a thousand times the losses it sustained.

This last boast, which expressed the morality of exacting hundreds of eyes for an eye and thousands of teeth for a tooth, seemed particularly repulsive in the mouth of a cheerleader for a theocratic State where an ethical elite claimed to provide inspired guidance on moral questions; but this will surprise only those uninformed about history's theocracies.

During this decade, the racism, the anti-Semitism to be more precise, of these admirers of the State of Israel became virulent. Zion's expropriated Semites were no longer considered human beings; they were Backward Arabs; only those among them who had been turned into good assimilated Israelis could be called human; the others were dirty Primitives. And Primitives, in the definition given a few centuries earlier by Conquistadores, not only had no right to resist humiliation, expropriation and desolation; Primitives had no right to exist; they only squandered nature's resources, they didn't know what to do with God's precious gifts! Only God's chosen knew how to use the Great Father's gifts, and they knew exactly what to do with them.

Yet even while dwelling on the backwardness of the expropriated, the cheerleaders became paranoid and pictured the pathetic resistance of the expropriated as a vast conspiracy of untold power and nearly cosmic scope.

Sartre's expression *mauvaise foi** is too weak to characterize the posture chosen by these people, but it's not my concern to coin another expression.

* * *

I survived into my forties, thanks partly to the fact that America still hadn't exterminated itself and the rest of humanity with the high-powered incinerants and poisons with which it was mining,** or rather undermining, its own as well as other people's lands.

This decade combined what I had earlier thought uncombinable; it combined a barrage of revelations about the Holocaust, in the form of movies, plays, books and articles, with the Pogrom perpetrated on Levantine Semites in Beirut by the State of Israel.***

The revelations touched the Holocaust in Vietnam only marginally; maybe two generations have to pass before such filth is hung out to air. The revelations were almost all about the Holocaust I had narrowly escaped as a child.

People who don't understand human freedom might think the terrible revelations could have only one effect, they could only turn people against the perpetrators of such atrocities, they could only make people empathize with the victims, they could only contribute to a resolve to abolish the very possibility of a repeat of such dehumanizing persecution and cold-blooded murder. But, for better or worse, such experiences, whether personally lived or learned from revelations, are nothing but the field over which human freedom soars like a bird of prey. The revelations about the forty-year-old Pogrom have even been turning up as justifications for a present-day Pogrom.

Pogrom is a Russian word that used to refer, in past years that now seem almost benign, to a riot of cudgel-armed men against poorly armed villagers with different cultural traits; the more heavily the State was involved in the riot, the more heinous was the Pogrom. The overwhelmingly stronger attackers projected their own character as bullies onto their weaker

*The usual English translation is "Bad faith."
**Mining, in the sense of setting explosive mines, making earth lethal.
***Written in mid-August, this statement referred to Israel's invasion and not yet to the Pogrom in the strict 19th century sense perpetrated in September. *(Sept. 16-18, 1982, to be exact)*

victims, convincing themselves that their victims were rich, powerful, well-armed and allied with the Devil. The attackers also projected their own violence onto their victims, constructing stories of the victims' brutality out of details taken from their own repertory of deeds. In nineteenth century Russia, a Pogrom was considered particularly violent if fifty people were killed.

The statistics underwent a complete metamorphosis in the twentieth century, when the State became the main rioter. The statistics of modern German and Russian and Turkish state-run Pogroms are known; the statistics from Vietnam and Beirut are not public yet.

Beirut and its inhabitants had already been made desolate by the presence of the violent resistance movement of the expropriated refugees ousted from Zion; if the casualties of those clashes were added to the number killed by the State of Israel's direct involvement in the riot—but I'll stop this; I don't want to play numbers games.

The trick of declaring war against the armed resistance and then attacking the resisters' unarmed kin as well as the surrounding population with the most gruesome products of Death-Science—this trick is not new. American Pioneers were pioneers in this too; they made it standard practice to declare war on indigenous warriors and then to murder and burn villages with only women and children in them. This is already modern war, what we know as war against civilian populations; it has also been called, more candidly, mass murder or genocide.

Maybe I shouldn't be surprised that the perpetrators of a Pogrom portray themselves as the victims, in the present case as victims of the Holocaust.

Herman Melville noticed over a century ago, in his analysis of the metaphysics of Indian-hating, that those who made a full-time profession of hunting and murdering indigenous people of this continent always made themselves appear, even in their own eyes, as the victims of manhunts.

The use the Nazis made of the International Jewish Conspiracy is better known: during all the years of atrocities defying belief, the Nazis considered themselves the victimized.

It's as if the experience of being a victim gave exemption from human solidarity, as if it gave special powers, as if it gave a license to kill.

Maybe I shouldn't be surprised, but I can't keep myself from being angry, because such a posture is the posture of a *Salaud,* the posture of one who denies human freedom, who denies that he chooses himself as killer. The experience, whether personally lived or learned from revelations, explains and determines nothing; it is nothing but a phoney alibi.

Melville analyzed the moral integrity of the Indian-hater.

I'm talking about modern Pogromists, and more narrowly about cheerleaders for Pogroms. I'm talking about people who haven't personally killed fifty or five or even one human being.

I'm talking about America, where the quest is to immerse oneself in Paradise while avoiding any contact with its dirty work, where only a minority is still involved in the personal doing of the dirty work, where the vast majority are full-time voyeurs, peepers, professors, call them what you will.

Among the voyeurs, I'm concentrating on the voyeurs of Holocausts and Pogroms. I have to keep referring to what's on the screen because that's what's being watched. But my concern is with the watcher, with one who chooses himself a voyeur, specifically a voyeur of Holocausts, a cheerleader for death squads.

Mention the words Beirut and Pogrom in the same sentence to such a one, and he'll vomit all the morality inside him: he won't vomit much.

The likeliest response you'll get is a moronic chuckle and a cynical laugh.

I'm reminded of my uncle, the one who wasn't hit by a car, who at least had the shred of moral integrity to see what others saw and reject it, and I contrast my uncle with this person who either sees nothing at all, or who cynically affirms what he sees, cynically accepts himself.

If he's an intellectual, a professor, he'll respond with the exact equivalent of the moronic grin or the cynical laugh but with words; he'll bombard you with sophistries, half truths and outright lies which are perfectly transparent to him even as he utters them.

This is not an airy, wide-eyed idealist but a gross, down-to-earth property-oriented materialist with no illusions about what constitutes expropriation of what he calls Real Estate. Yet this real estate man will start telling you that the Levantine Zion is a Jewish Land and he'll point to a two-thousand year old Title.

He calls Hitler a madman for having claimed the Sudetenland was a German land because he totally rejects the rules that would have made it a German land. International peace treaties are included in his rules, violent expropriations are not.

Yet suddenly he pulls out a set of rules which, if he really accepted them, would pulverize the entire edifice of Real Property. If he really accepted such rules, he would be selling plots in Gdansk to Kashubians returning from exile, tracts in Michigan, Wisconsin and Minnesota to Ojibwas reappropriating their homeland, estates in Iran, Iraq and much of Turkey to homeward bound Indian Parsees, and he would even have to lease parts of Zion itself to Chinese descendants of Nestorian Christians, and to many others besides.

Such arguments have more affinity with the moronic chuckle than with the cynical laugh.

The cynical laugh translated into words would say: We (they always say We) We conquered the Primitives, expropriated them and ousted them; the expropriated are still resisting, and in the meantime We have acquired two generations who have no other home but Zion; being Realists, we know we can end the resistance once and for all by exterminating the expropriated.

Such cynicism without a shred of moral integrity might be realistic, but it might also turn out to be what C.W. Mills called Crackpot Realism, because the resistance might survive and spread and it might go on as long as the Irish.

There's yet another response, the response of the cudgel-armed Defense League bully who thinks the absence of a brown shirt makes him unrecognizable.

He clenches his fist or tightens his grip on his club and shouts: Traitor!

This response is the most ominous, for it claims that We are a club to which all are welcome, but the membership of some is mandatory.

In this usage, Traitor does not mean anti-Semite, since it is aimed at people who empathize with the plight of the current Semites. Traitor does not mean Pogromist, since it is aimed at people who still empathize with the victims of the Pogrom. This term is one of the few components of the vocabulary of a racist through the ages; it means: Traitor to the Race.

And here I reach the single element which the new anti-Semite had not yet shared with the old anti-Semite: *Gleichschaltung,* the totalitarian "synchronization" of all political activity and expression. The entire Race must march in step, to the same drumbeat; all are to obey.

The uniqueness of the condemned Eichmann becomes reduced to a difference in holiday ritual.

It seems to me that such goons are not preservers of the traditions of a persecuted culture. They're Conversos, but not to the Catholicism of Fernando y Isabela; they're Conversos to the political practice of the Fuehrer.

The long exile is over; the persecuted refugee at long last returns to Zion, but so badly scarred he's unrecognizable, he has completely lost his self; he returns as anti-Semite, as Pogromist, as mass murderer; the ages of exile and suffering are still included in his makeup, but only as self-justifications, and as a repertory of horrors to impose on Primitives and even on Earth herself.

* * *

I think I've now shown that the experience of the Holocaust, whether lived or peeped, does not in itself make an individual a critic of Pogroms, and also that it does not confer special powers or give anyone a license to kill or make someone a mass murderer.

But I haven't even touched the large question that is raised by all this: Can I begin to explain why someone chooses himself a mass murderer?

I think I can begin to answer. At the risk of plagiarizing Sartre's portrait of the old anti-Semite, I can at least try to point to one or two of the elements in the field of choice of the new anti-Semite.

I could start by noticing that the new anti-Semite is not really so different from any other TV-watcher, and that TV-watching is somewhere near the core of the choice (I include newspapers and movies under the abbreviation for "tell-a-vision").

What the watcher sees on the screen are some of the "interesting" deeds, sifted and censored, of the monstrous ensemble in which he plays a trivial but daily role. The central but not often televized activity of this vast ensemble is industrial and clerical labor, forced labor, or just simply labor, the *Arbeit* which *macht frei.* *

*"Work Liberates": a slogan posted at the entrance to Nazi slave labor camps.

Solzhenitsyn, in his multi-volumed *Gulag Archipelago,* gave a profound analysis of what such *Arbeit* does to a human individual's outer and inner life; a comparably profound analysis has yet to be made of the administration that "synchronizes" the activity, the training institutions that produce the Eichmanns and Chemists who apply rational means to the perpetration of the irrational ends of their superiors.

I can't summarize Solzhenitsyn's findings; his books have to be read. In a brief space I can only say that the part of life spent in *Arbeit,* the triviality of existence in a commodity market as seller or customer, worker or client, leaves an individual without kinship or community or meaning; it dehumanizes him, evacuates him; it leaves nothing inside but the trivia that make up his outside. He no longer has the centrality, the significance, the self-powers given to all their members by ancient communities that no longer exist. He doesn't even have the phoney centrality given by religions which preserved a memory of the ancient qualities while reconciling people to worlds where those qualities were absent. Even the religions have been evacuated, pared down to empty rituals whose meaning has long been lost.

The gap is always there; it's like hunger: it hurts. Yet nothing seems to fill it.

Ah, but there's something that does fill it or at least seems to; it may be sawdust and not grated cheese, but it gives the stomach the illusion that it's been fed; it may be a total abdication of self-powers, a self-annihilation, but it creates the illusion of self-fulfillment, of reappropriation of the lost self-powers.

This something is the Told Vision which can be watched on off hours, and preferably all the time.

By choosing himself a Voyeur, the individual can *watch* everything he no longer *is.*

All the self-powers he no longer has, It has. And It has even more powers; It has powers no individual ever had; It has the power to turn deserts into forests and forests into deserts; It has the power to annihilate peoples and cultures who have survived since the beginning of time and to leave no trace that they ever existed; It even has the power to resuscitate the vanished peoples and cultures and endow them with eternal life in the conditioned air of museums.

In case the reader hasn't already guessed, It is the technological ensemble, the industrial process, the Messiah called Progress. It is America.

The individual deprived of meaning chooses to take the final leap into meaninglessness by identifying with the very process that deprives him. He becomes We, the exploited identifying with the exploiter. Henceforth his powers are Our powers, the powers of the ensemble, the powers of the alliance of workers with their own bosses known as the Developed Nation. The powerless individual becomes an essential switch in the all-powerful, all-knowing, all-seeing God, the central computer; he becomes one with the machine.

His immersion becomes an orgy during the crusades against those who are still outside the machine: untouched trees, wolves, Primitives.

During such crusades he becomes one of the last Pioneers; he joins hands across the centuries with the Conquistadores of the southern part and the Pioneers of the northern part of this double continent; he joins hands with Indian-haters and Discoverers and Crusaders; he feels America running in his veins at last, the America that was already brewing in the cauldrons of European Alchemists long before Colón (the Converso) reached the Caribs, Raleigh the Algonquians or Cartier the Iroquoians; he gives the coup de grace to his remaining humanity by identifying with the process exterminating culture, nature and humanity.

If I went on I would probably come to results already found by W. Reich in his study of the mass psychology of Fascism. It galls me that a new Fascism should choose to use the experience of the victims of the earlier Fascism among its justifications.

1982

The Continuing Appeal of Nationalism

Nationalism was proclaimed dead several times during the present century:

— after the first world war, when the last empires of Europe, the Austrian and the Turkish, were broken up into self-determined nations, and no deprived nationalists remained, except the Zionists;

— after the Bolshevik coup d'état, when it was said that the bourgeoisie's struggles for self-determination were henceforth superseded by struggles of workingmen, who had no country;

— after the military defeat of Fascist Italy and National Socialist Germany, when the genocidal corollaries of nationalism had been exhibited for all to see, when it was thought that nationalism as creed and as practice was permanently discredited.

Yet forty years after the military defeat of Fascists and National Socialists, we can see that nationalism did not only survive but was born again, underwent a revival. Nationalism has been revived not only by the so-called right, but also and primarily by the so-called left. After the national socialist war, nationalism ceased to be confined to conservatives, became the creed and practice of revolutionaries, and proved itself to be the only revolutionary creed that actually worked.

Leftist or revolutionary nationalists insist that their nationalism has nothing in common with the nationalism of fascists and national socialists, that theirs is a nationalism of the oppressed, that it offers personal as well as cultural liberation. The claims of the revolutionary nationalists have been broadcast to the world by the two oldest continuing hierarchic institutions surviving into our times: the Chinese State and, more recently, the Catholic Church. Currently nationalism is being touted as a strategy, science and theology of liberation, as a fulfillment of the Enlightenment's dictum that knowledge is power, as a proven answer to the question What Is to be Done.

To challenge these claims, and to see them in a context, I have to ask what nationalism is — not only the new revolutionary nationalism but also the old conservative one. I cannot start by defining the term, because nationalism is not a word with a static definition; it is a term that covers a sequence of different historical experiences. I'll start by giving a brief sketch of some of those experiences.

According to a common (and manipulable) misconception, imperialism is relatively recent, consists of the colonization of the entire world, and is the last stage of capitalism. This diagnosis points to a specific cure: nationalism is offered as the antidote to imperialism; wars of national liberation are said to break up the capitalist empire.

This diagnosis serves a purpose, but it does not describe any event or situation. We come closer to the truth when we stand this conception on its head and say that imperialism was the first stage of capitalism, that the world was subsequently colonized by nation-states, and that nationalism is the dominant, the current, and (hopefully) the last stage of capitalism. The facts of the case were not discovered yesterday; they are as familiar as the misconception that denies them.

It has been convenient, for various good reasons, to forget that, until recent centuries, the dominant powers of Eurasia were not nation-states but empires. A Celestial Empire ruled by the Ming dynasty, an Islamic Empire ruled by the Ottoman dynasty and a Catholic Empire ruled by the Hapsburg dynasty vied with each other for possession of the known world. Of the three, the Catholics were not the first imperialists but the last. The Celestial Empire of the Mings ruled over most of eastern Asia and had dispatched vast commercial fleets overseas a century before sea-borne Catholics invaded Mexico.

The celebrants of the Catholic feat forget that, between 1420 and 1430, Chinese imperial bureaucrat Cheng Ho commanded naval expeditions of 70,000 men and sailed, not only to nearby Malaya, Indonesia and Ceylon, but as far from home ports as the Persian Gulf, the Red Sea and Africa. The celebrants of Catholic conquistadores also belittle the imperial feats of the Ottomans, who conquered all but the westernmost provinces of the former Roman Empire, ruled over North Africa, Arabia, the Middle East and half of Europe, controlled the Mediterranean and hammered on the gates of Vienna. The imperial Catholics set out westward, beyond the boundaries of the known world, in order to escape from encirclement.

Nevertheless, it was the imperial Catholics who "discovered America," and their genocidal destruction and plunder of their "discovery" changed the balance of forces among Eurasia's empires.

Would imperial Chinese or Turks have been less lethal had they "discovered America"? All three empires regarded aliens as less than human and therefore as legitimate prey. The Chinese considered others barbarians; the Muslims and Catholics considered others unbelievers. The term unbeliever is not as brutal as the term barbarian, since an unbeliever ceases to be legitimate prey and becomes a full-fledged human by the simple act of converting to the true faith, whereas a barbarian remains prey until she or he is made over by the civilizer.

The term unbeliever, and the morality behind it, conflicted with the practice of the Catholic invaders. The contradiction between professions and acts was spotted by a very early critic, a priest called Las Casas, who noted that the conversion ceremonies were pretexts for separating and exterminating the unconverted, and that the converts themselves were not treated as fellow Catholics but as slaves.

The critiques of Las Casas did little more than embarrass the Catholic Church and Emperor. Laws were passed and investigators were dispatched, but to little effect, because the two aims of the Catholic expeditions, conversion and plunder, were contradictory. Most churchmen reconciled themselves to saving the gold and damning the souls. The Catholic Emperor increasingly depended on the plundered wealth to pay for the imperial household, army, and for the fleets that carried the plunder.

Plunder continued to take precedence over conversion, but the Catholics continued to be embarrassed. Their ideology was not altogether suited to their practice. The Catholics made much of their conquests of Aztecs and Incas, whom they described as empires with institutions similar to those of the Hapsburg Empire and with religious practices as demonic as those of the official enemy, the heathen empire of the Ottoman

Turks. But the Catholics did not make much of the wars of extermination against communities that had neither emperors nor standing armies. Such feats, although perpetrated regularly, conflicted with the ideology and were less than heroic.

The contradiction between the invaders' professions and their acts was not resolved by the imperial Catholics. It was resolved by harbingers of a new social form, the nation-state. Two harbingers appeared during the same year, 1561, when one of the Emperor's overseas adventurers proclaimed his independence from the empire, and several of the Emperor's bankers and provisioners launched a war of independence.

The overseas adventurer, Lope de Aguirre, failed to mobilize support and was executed.

The Emperor's bankers and provisioners mobilized the inhabitants of several imperial provinces and succeeded in severing the provinces from the empire (provinces which were later called Holland).

These two events were not yet struggles of national liberation. They were harbingers of things to come. They were also reminders of things past. In the bygone Roman Empire, Praetorian guards had been engaged to protect the Emperor; the guards had assumed ever more of the Emperor's functions and had eventually wielded the imperial power instead of the Emperor. In the Arabic Islamic Empire, the Caliph had engaged Turkish bodyguards to protect his person; the Turkish guards, like the earlier Praetorians, had assumed ever more of the Caliph's functions and had eventually taken over the imperial palace as well as the imperial office.

Lope de Aguirre and the Dutch grandees were not the Hapsburg monarch's bodyguards, but the Andean colonial adventurer and the Dutch commercial and financial houses did wield important imperial functions. These rebels, like the earlier Roman and Turkish guards, wanted to free themselves of the spiritual indignity and material burden of serving the Emperor; they already wielded the Emperor's powers; the Emperor was nothing more to them than a parasite.

Colonial adventurer Aguirre was apparently inept as a rebel; his time had not yet come.

The Dutch grandees were not inept, and their time had come. They did not overthrow the empire; they rationalized it. The Dutch commercial and financial houses already possessed much of the New World's wealth; they had received it as payment for provisioning the Emperor's fleets, armies and household. They now set out to plunder colonies in their own name and for their own benefit, unshackled by a parasitic overlord. And since they were not Catholics but Calvinist Protestants, they were not embarrassed by any contradiction between professions and acts. They made no profession of saving souls. Their Calvinism told them that an inscrutable God had saved or damned all souls at the beginning of Time and no Dutch priest could alter God's plan.

The Dutch were not crusaders; they confined themselves to unheroic, humorless, businesslike plunder, calculated and regularized; the plundering fleets departed and returned on schedule. The fact that the plundered aliens were unbelievers became less important than the fact that they were not Dutchmen.

West Eurasian forerunners of nationalism coined the term savages. This term was a synonym of the east Eurasian Celestial Empire's term barbarians. Both terms designated human beings as legitimate prey.

During the following two centuries, the invasions, subjugations and expropriations initiated by the Hapsburgs were imitated by other European royal houses.

Seen through the lenses of nationalist historians, the initial colonizers as well as their later imitators look like nations: Spain, Holland, England, France. But seen from a vantage point in the past, the colonizing powers are Hapsburgs, Tudors, Stuarts, Bourbons, Oranges — namely dynasties identical to the dynastic families that had been feuding for wealth and power ever since the fall of the western Roman empire. The invaders can be seen from both vantage points because a transition was taking place. The entities were no longer mere feudal estates, but they were not yet full-fledged nations; they already possessed some, but not yet all, the attributes of a nation-state. The most notable missing element was the national army. Tudors and Bourbons already manipulated the Englishness or Frenchness of their subjects, especially during wars against another monarch's subjects. But neither Scots and Irishmen, nor Corsicans and Provençals, were recruited to fight and die for "the love of their country." War was an onerous feudal burden, a corvée; the only volunteers were adventurers who dreamt of gold; the only patriots were patriots of Eldorado.

The tenets of what was going to become the nationalist creed did not appeal to the ruling dynasts, who clung to their own tried and tested tenets. The new tenets appealed to the dynast's higher servants, his money-lenders, spice-vendors, military suppliers and colony-plunderers. These people, like Lope de Aguirre and the Dutch grandees, like earlier Roman and Turkish guards, wielded key functions yet remained servants. Many if not most of them burned to shake off the indignity and the burden, to rid themselves of the parasitic overlord, to carry on the exploitation of countrymen and the plunder of colonials in their own name and for their own benefit.

Later known as the bourgeoisie or the middle class, these people had become rich and powerful since the days of the first westward-bound fleets. A portion of their wealth had come from the plundered colonies, as payment for the services they had sold to the Emperor; this sum of wealth would later be called a primitive accumulation of capital. Another portion of their wealth had come from the plunder of their own local countrymen and neighbors by a method later known as capitalism; the method was not altogether new, but it became very widespread after the middle classes got their hands on the New World's silver and gold.

These middle classes wielded important powers, but they were not yet experienced in wielding the central political power. In England they overthrew a monarch and proclaimed a commonwealth but, fearing that the popular energies they had mobilized against the upper class could turn against the middle class, they soon restored another monarch of the same dynastic house.

Nationalism did not really come into its own until the late 1700s when two explosions, thirteen years apart, reversed the relative standing of the two upper classes and permanently changed the political geography of the globe. In 1776, colonial merchants and adventurers reenacted Aguirre's feat of proclaiming their independence from the ruling overseas dynast, outdid their predecessor by mobilizing their fellow-settlers, and succeeded in severing themselves from the Hanoverian British Empire. And in 1789, enlightened merchants and scribes outdid their Dutch forerunners by mobilizing, not a few outlying provinces, but the entire subject population, by overthrowing and slaying the ruling Bourbon monarch, and by remaking all feudal bonds into national bonds. These two events marked the end of an era. Henceforth even the surviving dynasts hastily or gradually became nationalists, and the remaining royal estates took on ever more of the attributes of nation-states.

The two eighteenth century revolutions were very different, and they contributed different and even conflicting elements to the creed and practice of nationalism. I do not intend to analyze these events here, but only to remind the reader of some of the elements.

Both rebellions successfully broke the bonds of fealty to a monarchic house, and both ended with the establishment of capitalist nation-states, but between the first act and the last they had little in common. The main animators of both revolts were familiar with the rationalistic doctrines of the Enlightenment, but the self-styled Americans confined themselves to political problems, largely to the problem of establishing a state machinery that could take up where King George left off. Many of the French went much further; they posed the problem of restructuring not only the state but all of society; they challenged not only the bond of subject to monarch, but also the bond of slave to master, a bond that remained sacred to the Americans. Both groups were undoubtedly familiar with Jean-Jacques Rousseau's observation that human beings were born free, yet everywhere were bound in chains, but the French understood the chains more profoundly and made a greater effort to break them.

As influenced by rationalistic doctrines as Rousseau himself had been, French revolutionaries tried to apply social reason to the human environment in the same way that natural reason, or science, was starting to be applied to the natural environment.

Rousseau had worked at his desk; he had tried to establish social justice on paper, by entrusting human affairs to an entity that embodied the general will. The revolutionaries agitated to establish social justice not only on paper, but in the midst of mobilized and armed human beings, many of them enraged, most of them poor.

Rousseau's abstract entity took the concrete form of a Committee of Public Safety (or Public Health), a police organization that considered itself the embodiment of the general will. The virtuous committee members conscientiously applied the findings of reason to human affairs. They considered themselves the nation's surgeons. They carved their personal obsessions into society by means of the state's razor blade.

The application of science to the environment took the form of systematic terror. The instrument of Reason and Justice was the guillotine.

The Terror decapitated the former rulers and then turned on the revolutionaries.

Fear stimulated a reaction that swept away the Terror as well as the Justice. The mobilized energy of bloodthirsty patriots was sent abroad, to impose enlightenment on foreigners by force, to expand the nation into an empire. The provisioning of national armies was far more lucrative than the provisioning of feudal armies ever had been, and former revolutionaries became rich and powerful members of the middle class, which was now the top class, the ruling class. The terror as well as the wars bequeathed a fateful legacy to the creed and practice of later nationalisms.

The legacy of the American revolution was of an altogether different kind. The Americans were less concerned with justice, more concerned with property.

The settler-invaders of the northern continent's eastern shore needed George of Hanover no more urgently than Lope de Aguirre had needed Philip of Hapsburg. Or rather, the rich and powerful among the settlers needed King George's apparatus to protect their wealth, but not to gain it. If they could organize a repressive apparatus on their own, they would not need King George at all.

Confident of their ability to launch an apparatus of their own, the colonial slave-holders, land-speculators, produce-exporters and bankers found the King's taxes and acts intolerable. The most intolerable of the King's acts was the act that temporarily banned unauthorized incursions into the lands of the continent's original inhabitants; the King's advisers had their eyes on the animal furs supplied by indigenous hunters; the revolutionary land-speculators had theirs on the hunters' lands.

Unlike Aguirre, the federated colonizers of the north succeeded in establishing their own independent repressive apparatus, and they did this by stirring up a minimum of cravings for justice; their aim was to overthrow the King's power, not their own. Rather than rely excessively on their less fortunate fellow-settlers or backwoods squatters, not to speak of their slaves, these revolutionaries relied on mercenaries and on indispensable aid from the Bourbon monarch who would be overthrown a few years later by more virtuous revolutionaries.

The North American colonizers broke the traditional bonds of fealty and feudal obligation but, unlike the French, they only gradually replaced the traditional bonds with bonds of patriotism and nationhood. They were not quite a nation; their reluctant mobilization of the colonial countryside had not fused them into one, and the multi-lingual, multi-cultural and socially divided underlying population resisted such a fusion. The new repressive apparatus was not tried and tested, and it did not command the undivided loyalty of the underlying population, which was not yet patriotic. Something else was needed. Slave-masters who had overthrown their king feared that their slaves could similarly overthrow the masters; the insurrection in Haiti made this fear less than hypothetical. And although they no longer feared being pushed into the sea by the continent's indigenous inhabitants, the traders and speculators worried about their ability to thrust further into the continent's interior.

The American settler-invaders had recourse to an instrument that was not, like the guillotine, a new invention, but that was just as lethal. This instrument would later be called Racism, and it would become embedded in nationalist practice. Racism, like later products of practical Americans, was a pragmatic principle; its content was not important; what mattered was the fact that it worked.

Human beings were mobilized in terms of their lowest and most superficial common denominator, and they responded. People who had abandoned their villages and families, who were forgetting their languages and losing their cultures, who were all but depleted of their sociability, were manipulated into considering their skin color a substitute for all they had lost. They were made proud of something that was neither a personal feat nor even, like language, a personal acquisition. They were fused into a nation of white men. (White women and children existed only as scalped victims, as proofs of the bestiality of the hunted prey.) The extent of the depletion is revealed by the nonentities the white men shared with each other: white blood, white thoughts, and membership in a white race. Debtors, squatters and servants, as white men, had everything in common with bankers, land speculators and plantation owners, nothing in common with Redskins, Blackskins or Yellowskins. Fused by such a principle, they could also be mobilized by it, turned into white mobs, lynch mobs, "Indian fighters."

Racism had initially been one among several methods of mobilizing colonial armies, and although it was exploited more fully in America than it ever had been before, it did not supplant the other methods but rather supplemented them. The victims of the invading pioneers were still described as unbelievers, as heathen. But the pioneers, like the earlier Dutch, were largely Protestant Christians, and they regarded heathenism as something to be punished, not remedied. The victims also continued to be designated as savages, cannibals and primitives, but these terms, too, ceased to be diagnoses of conditions that could be remedied, and tended to become synonyms of non-white, a condition that could not be remedied. Racism was an ideology perfectly suited to a practice of enslavement and extermination.

The lynch-mob approach, the ganging-up on victims defined as inferior, appealed to bullies whose humanity was stunted and who lacked any notion of fair play. But this approach did not appeal to everyone. American businessmen, part hustlers and part confidence men, always had something for everyone. For the numerous Saint Georges with some notion of honor and great thirst for heroism, the enemy was depicted somewhat differently; for them there were nations as rich and powerful as their own in the trans-montane woodlands and on the shores of the Great Lakes.

The celebrants of the heroic feats of imperial Spaniards had found empires in central Mexico and on top of the Andes. The celebrants of nationalist American heroes found nations; they transformed desperate resistances of an-archic villagers into international conspiracies masterminded by military archons such as General Pontiac and General Tecumseh; they peopled the woodlands with formidable national leaders, efficient general staffs, and armies of uncountable patriotic troops; they projected their own repressive structures into the unknown; they saw an exact copy of themselves, with all the colors reversed — something like a photographic negative. The enemy thus became an equal in terms of structure, power and aims. War against such an enemy was not only fair play; it was a dire necessity, a matter of life and death. The enemy's other attributes — the heathenism, the savagery, the cannibalism — made the tasks of expropriating, enslaving and exterminating all the more urgent, made these feats all the more heroic.

The repertory of the nationalist program was now more or less complete. This statement might baffle a reader who cannot yet see any "real nations" in the field. The United States was still a collection of multi-lingual, multi-religious and multi-cultural "ethnicities," and the French nation had overflowed its boundaries and turned itself into a Napoleonic empire. The reader might be trying to apply a definition of a nation as an organized territory consisting of people who share a common language, religion and customs, or at least one of the three. Such a definition, clear, pat and static, is not a description of the phenomenon but an apology for it, a justification. The phenomenon was not a static definition but a dynamic process. The common language, religion and customs, like the white blood of the American colonizers, were mere pretexts, instruments for mobilizing armies. The culmination of the process was not an enshrinement of the commonalities, but a depletion, a total loss of language, religion and customs; the inhabitants of a nation spoke the language of capital, worshipped on the altar of the state and confined their customs to those permitted by the national police.

Nationalism is the opposite of imperialism only in the realm of definitions. In practice, nationalism was a methodology for conducting the empire of capital.

The continual increase of capital, often referred to as material progress, economic development or industrialization, was the main activity of the middle classes, the so-called bourgeoisie, because capital was what they owned, it was their property; the upper classes owned estates.

The discovery of new worlds of wealth had enormously enriched these middle classes, but had also made them vulnerable. The kings and nobles who initially gathered the new world's plundered wealth resented losing all but a few trophies to their middle class merchants. This could not be helped. The wealth did not arrive in usable forms; the merchants supplied the king with things he could use, in exchange for the plundered treasures. Even so, monarchs who saw themselves grow poor while their merchants grew rich were not above using their armed retainers to plunder the wealthy merchants. Consequently the middle classes suffered continual injuries under the old regime — injuries to their property. The king's army and police were not reliable protectors of middle class property, and the powerful merchants, who already operated the business of the empire, took measures to put an end to the instability; they took the politics in hand as well. They could have hired private armies, and they often did. But as soon as instruments for mobilizing national armies and national police forces appeared on the horizon, the injured businessmen had recourse to them. The main virtue of a national armed force is that it guarantees that a patriotic servant will war alongside his own boss against an enemy boss's servant.

The stability assured by a national repressive apparatus gave the owners something like a hothouse in which their capital could grow, increase, multiply. The term "grow" and its corollaries come from the capitalists' own vocabulary. These people think of a unit of capital as a grain or seed which they invest in fertile soil. In spring they see a plant grow from each seed. In summer they harvest so many seeds from each plant that, after paying for the soil, sunshine and rain, they still have more seeds than they had initially. The following year they enlarge their field, and gradually the whole countryside becomes improved. In reality, the initial "grains" are money; the sunshine and rain are the expended energies of laborers; the plants are factories, workshops and mines, the harvested fruits are commodities, bits of processed world; and the excess or additional grains, the profits, are emoluments which the capitalist keeps for himself instead of dividing them up among the workers.

The process as a whole consisted of the processing of natural substances into saleable items or commodities, and of the incarceration of wage workers in the processing plants.

The marriage of Capital with Science was responsible for the great leap forward into what we live in today. Pure scientists discovered the components into which the natural environment could be decomposed; investors placed their bets on the various methods of decomposition; applied scientists or managers saw to it that the wage workers in their charge carried the project through. Social scientists sought ways to make the workers less human, more efficient and machine-like. Thanks to science, capitalists were able to transform much of the natural environment into a processed world, an artifice, and to reduce most human beings into efficient tenders of the artifice.

The process of capitalist production was analyzed and criticized by many philosophers and poets, most notably by Karl Marx,[1] whose critiques animated, and continue to animate, militant social movements. Marx had a significant blind spot; most of his disciples, and many militants who were not his disciples, built their platforms on that blind spot. Marx was an enthusiastic supporter of the bourgeoisie's struggle for liberation from feudal bonds — who was not an enthusiast in those days? He, who observed that the ruling ideas of an epoch were the ideas of the ruling class, shared many of the ideas of the newly empowered middle class. He was an enthusiast of the Enlightenment, of rationalism, of material progress. It was Marx who insightfully pointed out that every time a worker reproduced his labor power, every minute he devoted to his assigned task, he enlarged the material and social apparatus that dehumanized him. Yet the same Marx was an enthusiast for the application of science to production.

Marx made a thorough analysis of the production process as an exploitation of labor, but he made only cursory and reluctant comments about the prerequisite for capitalist production, about the initial capital that made the process possible.[2] Without the initial capital, there could have been no investments, no production, no great leap forward. This prerequisite was analyzed by the early Soviet Russian marxist Preobrazhensky, who borrowed several insights from the Polish marxist Rosa Luxemburg to formulate his theory of primitive accumulation.[3] By primitive, Preobrazhensky meant the basement of the capitalist edifice, the foundation, the prerequisite. This prerequisite cannot emerge from the capitalist production process itself, if that process is not yet under way. It must, and does, come from outside the production process. It comes from the plundered colonies. It comes from the expropriated and exterminated populations of the colonies. In earlier days, when there were no overseas colonies, the first capital, the prerequisite for capitalist production, had been squeezed out of internal colonies, out of plundered peasants whose lands were enclosed and crops requisitioned, out of expelled Jews and Muslims whose possessions were expropriated.

The primitive or preliminary accumulation of capital is not something that happened once, in the distant past, and never after. It is something that continues to accompany the capitalist production process, and is an integral part of it. The process described by Marx is responsible for the regular and expected profits; the process described by Preobrazhensky is responsible for the takeoffs, the windfalls and the great leaps forward. The regular profits are periodically destroyed by crises endemic to the system; new injections of preliminary capital are the only known cure to the crises. Without an ongoing primitive accumulation of capital, the production process would stop; each crisis would tend to become permanent.

Genocide, the rationally calculated extermination

of human populations designated as legitimate prey, has not been an aberration in an otherwise peaceful march of progress. Genocide has been a prerequisite of that progress. This is why national armed forces were indispensable to the wielders of capital. These forces did not only protect the owners of capital from the insurrectionary wrath of their own exploited wage workers. These forces also captured the holy grail, the magic lantern, the preliminary capital, by battering the gates of resisting or unresisting outsiders, by looting, deporting and murdering.

The footprints of the national armies are the traces of the march of progress. These patriotic armies were, and still are, the seventh wonder of the world. In them, the wolf lay alongside the lamb, the spider alongside the fly. In them, exploited workers were the chums of exploiters, indebted peasants the chums of creditors, suckers the chums of hustlers in a companionship stimulated not by love but by hatred — hatred of potential sources of preliminary capital designated as unbelievers, savages, inferior races.

Human communities as variegated in their ways and beliefs as birds are in feathers were invaded, despoiled and at last exterminated beyond imagination's grasp. The clothes and artifacts of the vanished communities were gathered up as trophies and displayed in museums as additional traces of the march of progress; the extinct beliefs and ways became the curiosities of yet another of the invaders' many sciences. The expropriated fields, forests and animals were garnered as bonanzas, as preliminary capital, as the precondition for the production process that was to turn the fields into farms, the trees into lumber, the animals into hats, the minerals into munitions, the human survivors into cheap labor. Genocide was, and still is, the precondition, the cornerstone and groundwork of the military-industrial complexes, of the processed environments, of the worlds of offices and parking lots.

Nationalism was so perfectly suited to its double task, the domestication of workers and the despoliation of aliens, that it appealed to everyone — everyone, that is, who wielded or aspired to wield a portion of capital.

During the nineteenth century, especially during its second half, every owner of investable capital discovered that he had roots among the mobilizable countryfolk who spoke his mother's tongue and worshipped his father's gods. The fervor of such a nationalist was transparently cynical, since he was the countryman who no longer had roots among his mother's or father's kin: he found his salvation in his savings, prayed to his investments and spoke the language of cost accounting. But he had learned, from Americans and Frenchmen, that although he could not mobilize the countryfolk as loyal servants, clients and customers, he could mobilize them as loyal fellow-Italians, Greeks or Germans, as loyal fellow-Catholics, Orthodox or Protestants. Languages, religions and customs became welding materials for the construction of nation-states.

The welding materials were means, not ends. The purpose of the national entities was not to develop languages, religions or customs, but to develop national economies, to turn the countryfolk into workers and soldiers, to turn the motherland into mines and factories, to turn dynastic estates into capitalist enterprises. Without the capital, there could be no munitions or supplies, no national army, no nation.

Savings and investments, market research and cost accounting, the obsessions of the rationalistic former middle classes, became the ruling obsessions. These rationalistic obsessions became not only sovereign but also exclusive. Individuals who enacted other obsessions, irrational ones, were put away in madhouses, asylums.

The nations usually were but need no longer have been monotheistic; the former god or gods had lost their importance except as welding materials. The nations were mono-obsessive, and if monotheism served the ruling obsession, then it too was mobilized.

World War I marked the end of one phase of the nationalizing process, the phase that had begun with the American and French revolutions, the phase that had been announced much earlier by the declaration of Aguirre and the revolt of the Dutch grandees. The conflicting claims of old and newly-constituted nations were in fact the causes of that war. Germany, Italy and Japan, as well as Greece, Serbia and colonial Latin

America, had already taken on most of the attributes of their nationalistic predecessors, had become national empires, monarchies and republics, and the more powerful of the new arrivals aspired to take on the main missing attribute, the colonial empire. During that war, all the mobilizable components of the two remaining dynastic empires, the Ottoman and the Hapsburg, constituted themselves into nations. When bourgeoisies with different languages and religions, such as Turks and Armenians, claimed the same territory, the weaker were treated like so-called American Indians; they were exterminated. National Sovereignty and Genocide were — and still are — corollaries.

Common language and religion appear to be corollaries of nationhood, but only because of an optical illusion. As welding materials, languages and religions were used when they served their purpose, discarded when they did not. Neither multi-lingual Switzerland nor multi-religious Yugoslavia were banned from the family of nations. The shapes of noses and the color of hair could also have been used to mobilize patriots — and later were. The shared heritages, roots and commonalities had to satisfy only one criterion, the criterion of American-style pragmatic reason: did they work? Whatever worked was used. The shared traits were important, not because of their cultural, historical or philosophical content, but because they were useful for organizing a police to protect the national property and for mobilizing an army to plunder the colonies.

Once a nation was constituted, human beings who lived on the national territory but did not possess the national traits could be transformed into internal colonies, namely into sources of preliminary capital. Without preliminary capital, no nation could become a great nation, and nations that aspired to greatness but lacked adequate overseas colonies could resort to plundering, exterminating and expropriating those of their countrymen who did not possess the national traits.

The establishment of nation-states was greeted with euphoric enthusiasm by poets as well as peasants who thought their muses or their gods had at last descended to earth. The main wet blankets amidst the waving banners and flying confetti were the former rulers, the colonized, and the disciples of Karl Marx.

The overthrown and the colonized were unenthusiastic for obvious reasons.

The disciples of Marx were unenthusiastic because they had learned from the master that national liberation meant national exploitation, that the national government was the executive committee of the national capitalist class, that the nation had nothing for workingmen but chains. These strategists for the workingmen, who were not themselves workingmen but were as bourgeois as the ruling capitalists, proclaimed that the workingmen had no country and organized themselves into an International. This International split into three, and each International moved increasingly into the field of Marx's blind spot.

The First International was carried off by Marx's one-time Russian translator and then antagonist Bakunin, an inveterate rebel who had been a fervent nationalist until he'd learned about exploitation from Marx. Bakunin and his companions, rebels against all authorities, also rebelled against the authority of Marx; they suspected Marx of trying to turn the International into a state as repressive as the feudal and national combined. Bakunin and his followers were unambiguous in their rejection of all states, but they were ambiguous about capitalist enterprise. Even more than Marx, they glorified science, celebrated material progress and hailed industrialization. Being rebels, they considered every fight a good fight, but the best of all was the fight against the bourgeoisie's former enemies, the fight against feudal landlords and the Catholic Church. Thus the Bakuninist International flourished in places like Spain, where the bourgeoisie had not completed its struggle for independence but had, instead, allied itself with feudal barons and the Church for protection from insurgent workers and peasants. The Bakuninists fought to complete the bourgeois revolution without and against the bourgeoisie. They called themselves anarchists and disdained all states, but did not begin to explain how they would procure the preliminary or the subsequent industry, progress and science, namely the capital, without an army and a police. They were never given a real chance to resolve their contradiction in practice, and present day Bakuninists have still not resolved it, have not even become aware that there is a contradiction between anarchy and industry.

The Second International, less rebellious than the first, quickly came to terms with capital as well as the state. Solidly entrenched in Marx's blind spot, the professors of this organization did not become enmeshed in any Bakuninist contradiction. It was obvious to them that the exploitation and the plunder were necessary conditions for the material progress, and they realistically reconciled themselves to what could not be helped. All they asked for was a greater share of the benefits for the workingmen, and offices in the political establishment for themselves, as the workingmen's representatives. Like the good unionists who preceded and followed them, the socialist professors were embarrassed by "the colonial question," but their embarrassment, like Philip Hapsburg's, merely gave them bad consciences. In time, imperial German socialists, royal Danish socialists and republican French socialists even ceased to be internationalists.

The Third International did not only come to terms with capital and the state; it made them its goal. This international was not formed by rebellious or dissenting intellectuals; it was created by a state, the Russian state, after the Bolshevik Party installed itself in that state's offices. The main activity of this international was to advertise the feats of the revamped Russian state, of its ruling party, and of the party's founder, a man who called himself Lenin. The feats of that party and founder were indeed momentous, but the advertisers did their best to hide what was most momentous about them.

The first world war had left two vast empires in a quandry. The Celestial Empire of China, the oldest continuous state in the world, and the Empire of the Tsars, a much more recent operation, hovered shakily between the prospect of turning themselves into nation-states and the prospect of decomposing into smaller units, like their Ottoman and Hapsburg counterparts had done.

Lenin resolved this quandry for Russia. Is such a

thing possible? Marx had observed that a single individual could not change circumstances; he could only
avail himself of them. Marx was probably right. Lenin's
feat was not to change circumstances, but to avail
himself of them in an extraordinary manner. The feat
was monumental in its opportunism.

Lenin was a Russian bourgeois who cursed the
weakness and ineptitude of the Russian bourgeoisie. [4]
An enthusiast for capitalist development, an ardent ad-
mirer of American-style progress, he did not make common cause with those he cursed, but rather with their
enemies, with the anti-capitalist disciples of Marx. He
availed himself of Marx's blind spot to transform
Marx's critique of the capitalist production process into a manual for developing capital, a "how-to-do-it"
guide. Marx's studies of exploitation and immiseration
became food for the famished, a cornucopia, a virtual
horn of plenty. American businessmen had already
marketed urine as spring water, but no American confidence man had yet managed an inversion of such
magnitude.

No circumstances were changed. Every step of the
inversion was carried out with available circumstances, with tried and tested methods. Russian
countryfolk could not be mobilized in terms of their
Russianness or orthodoxy or whiteness, but they could
be, and were, mobilized in terms of their exploitation,
their oppression, their ages of suffering under the
despotism of the Tsars. Oppression and exploitation
became welding materials. The long sufferings under
the Tsars were used in the same way and for the same
purpose as the scalpings of white women and children
had been used by Americans; they were used to
organize people into fighting units, into embryos of the
national army and the national police.

The presentation of the dictator and of the Party's
central committee as a dictatorship of the liberated
proletariat seemed to be something new, but even this
was new only in the words that were used. This was
something as old as the Pharaohs and Lugals of ancient
Egypt and Mesopotamia, who had been chosen by the
god to lead the people, who had embodied the people in
their dialogues with the god. This was a tried and
tested gimmick of rulers. Even if the ancient precedents
were temporarily forgotten, a more recent precedent

had been provided by the French Committee of Public Health, which had presented itself as the embodiment of the nation's general will.

The goal, communism, the overthrow and supersession of capitalism, also seemed something new, seemed to be a change of circumstances. But only the word was new. The goal of the dictator of the proletariat was still American-style progress, capitalist development, electrification, rapid mass transportation, science, the processing of the natural environment. The goal was the capitalism that the weak and inept Russian bourgeoisie had failed to develop. With Marx's *Capital* as their light and guide, the dictator and his Party would develop capitalism in Russia; they would serve as a substitute bourgeoisie, and they would use the power of the state not only to police the process, but to launch and manage it as well.

Lenin did not live long enough to demonstrate his virtuosity as general manager of Russian capital, but his successor Stalin amply demonstrated the powers of the founder's machine. The first step was the primitive accumulation of capital. If Marx had not been very clear about this, Preobrazhensky had been very clear. Preobrazhensky was jailed, but his description of the tried and tested methods of procuring preliminary capital was applied to vast Russia. The preliminary capital of English, American, Belgian and other capitalists had come from plundered overseas colonies. Russia had no overseas colonies. This lack was no obstacle. The entire Russian countryside was transformed into a colony.

The first sources of preliminary capital were Kulaks, peasants who had something worth plundering. This drive was so successful that it was applied to the remaining peasants as well, with the rational expectation that small amounts plundered from many people would yield a substantial hoard.

The peasants were not the only colonials. The former ruling class had already been thoroughly expropriated of all its wealth and property, but yet other sources of preliminary capital were found. With the totality of state power concentrated in their hands, the dictators soon discovered that they could manufacture sources of primitive accumulation. Successful entrepreneurs, dissatisfied workers and peasants, militants of competing organizations, even disillusioned Party members, could be designated as counter-revolutionaries, rounded up, expropriated and shipped off to labor camps. All the deportations, mass executions and expropriations of earlier colonizers were re-enacted in Russia.

Earlier colonizers, being pioneers, had resorted to trial and error. The Russian dictators did not have to resort to trial and error. By their time, all the methods of procuring preliminary capital had been tried and tested, and could be scientifically applied. Russian capital developed in a totally controlled environment, a hothouse; every lever, every variable, was controlled by the national police. Functions which had been left to chance or to other bodies in less controlled environments fell to the police in the Russian hothouse. The fact that the colonials were not abroad but within, and therefore subject not to conquest but to arrest, further increased the role and size of the police. In time the omnipotent and omnipresent police became the visible emanation and embodiment of the proletariat, and communism became a synonym of total police organization and control.

Lenin's expectations were not, however, fully realized by the Russian hothouse. The police-as-capitalist worked wonders in procuring preliminary capital from expropriated counter-revolutionaries, but did not do nearly as well in managing the capitalist production process. It may still be too early to tell for sure, but to date this police bureaucracy has been at least as inept in this role as the bourgeoisie Lenin had cursed; its ability to discover ever new sources of preliminary capital seems to be all that has kept it afloat.

Nor has the appeal of this apparatus been on a level with Lenin's expectations. The Leninist police apparatus has not appealed to businessmen or to established politicians; it has not recommended itself as a superior method of managing the production process. It has appealed to a somewhat different social class, a class I will briefly try to describe, and it has recommended itself to this class primarily as a method of seizing national power and secondarily as a method of primitive accumulation of capital.

The heirs of Lenin and Stalin have not been actual

Praetorian guards, actual wielders of economic and political power in the name and for the benefit of a superfluous monarch; they have been understudy Praetorians, students of economic and political power who despaired of ever reaching even intermediate levels of power. The Leninist model has offered such people the prospect of leaping over the intermediate levels directly into the central palace.

The heirs of Lenin were clerks and minor officials, people like Mussolini, Mao Zedong and Hitler, people who, like Lenin himself, cursed their weak and inept bourgeoisies for having failed to establish their nation's greatness.

(I do not include the Zionists among the heirs of Lenin because they belong to an earlier generation. They were Lenin's contemporaries who had, perhaps independently, discovered the power of persecution and suffering as welding materials for the mobilization of a national army and police. The Zionists made other contributions of their own. Their treatment of a dispersed religious population as a nation, their imposition of the capitalist nation-state as that population's end-all and be-all, and their reduction of a religious heritage to a racial heritage, contributed significant elements to the nationalist methodology, and would have fateful consequences when they were applied on a population of Jews, not all of them Zionists, by a population welded together as a "German race.")

Mussolini, Mao Zedong and Hitler cut through the curtain of slogans and saw Lenin's and Stalin's feats for what they were: successful methods of seizing and maintaining state power. All three trimmed the methodology down to its essentials. The first step was to join up with likeminded students of power and to form the nucleus of the police organization, an outfit called, after Lenin's, the Party. The next step was to recruit the mass base, the available troops and troop suppliers. The third step was to seize the apparatus of the state, to install the theoretician in the office of Duce, Chairman or Fuehrer, to apportion police and managerial functions among the elite or cadre, and to put the mass base to work. The fourth step was to secure the preliminary capital needed to repair or launch a military-industrial complex capable of supporting the national leader and cadre, the police and army, the industrial managers; without this capital there could be no weapons, no power, no nation.

The heirs of Lenin and Stalin further trimmed the methodology, in their recruiting drives, by minimizing capitalist exploitation and by concentrating on national oppression. Talk of exploitation no longer served a purpose, and had in fact become embarrassing, since it was obvious to all, especially to wage workers, that successful revolutionaries had not put an end to wage labor, but had extended its domain.

Being as pragmatic as American businessmen, the new revolutionaries did not speak of liberation from wage labor, but of national liberation. [5] This type of liberation was not a dream of romantic utopians; it was precisely what was possible, and all that was possible, in the existing world; one needed only to avail oneself of already existing circumstances to make it happen. National liberation consisted of the liberation of the national chairman and the national police from the chains of powerlessness; the investiture of the chairman and the establishment of the police were not pipe dreams but components of a tried and tested strategy, a science.

Fascist and National Socialist Parties were the first to prove that the strategy worked, that the Bolshevik Party's feat could actually be repeated. The national chairmen and their staffs installed themselves in power and set out to procure the preliminary capital needed for national greatness. The Fascists thrust themselves into one of the last uninvaded regions of Africa and gouged it as earlier industrializers had gouged their colonial empires. The National Socialists targeted Jews, an inner population that had been members of a "unified Germany" as long as other Germans, as their first source of primitive accumulation because many of the Jews, like many of Stalin's Kulaks, had things worth plundering.

Zionists had already preceded the National Socialists in reducing a religion to a race, and National Socialists could look back to American pioneers for ways to use the instrument of racism. Hitler's elite needed only to translate the corpus of American racist research to equip their scientific institutes with large libraries. The National Socialists dealt with Jews much the same way as the Americans had earlier dealt with the indigenous population of North America, except that the National Socialists applied a later and much more powerful technology to the task of deporting, expropriating and exterminating human beings. But in this the later exterminators were not innovators; they merely availed themselves of the circumstances within their reach.

The Fascists and National Socialists were joined by Japanese empire-builders who feared that the decomposing Celestial Empire would become a source of preliminary capital for Russian or revolutionary Chinese industrializers. Forming an Axis, the three set out to turn the world's continents into sources of primitive accumulation of capital. They were not bothered by other nations until they started to encroach on the colonies and homelands of established capitalist powers. The reduction of already established capitalists to colonized prey could be practiced internally, where it was always legal since the nation's rulers make its laws — and had already been practiced internally by Leninists and Stalinists. But such a practice would have amounted to a change of circumstances, and it could not be carried abroad without provoking a world war. The Axis powers overreached themselves and lost.

After the war, many reasonable people would speak of the aims of the Axis as irrational and of Hitler as a lunatic. Yet the same reasonable people would consider men like George Washington and Thomas Jefferson sane and rational, even though these men envisioned and began to enact the conquest of a vast continent, the deportation and extermination of the continent's population, at a time when such a project was much less feasible than the project of the Axis.[6] It is true that the technologies as well as the physical, chemical, biological and social sciences applied by Washington and Jefferson were quite different from those applied by the National Socialists. But if knowledge is power, if it was rational for the earlier pioneers to maim and kill with gunpowder in the age of horse-drawn carriages, why was it irrational for National Socialists to maim and kill with high explosives, gas and chemical agents in the age of rockets, submarines and "freeways"?

The Nazis were, if anything, yet more

scientifically-oriented than the Americans. In their time, they were a synonym for scientific efficiency to much of the world. They kept files on everything, tabulated and cross tabulated their findings, published their tabulations in scientific journals. Among them, even racism was not the property of frontier rabble-rousers, but of well-endowed institutes.

Many reasonable people seem to equate lunacy with failure. This would not be the first time. Many called Napoleon a lunatic when he was in prison or in exile, but when Napoleon re-emerged as the Emperor, the same people spoke of him with respect, even reverence. Incarceration and exile are not only regarded as remedies for lunacy, but also as its symptoms. Failure is foolishness.

Mao Zedong, the third pioneering national socialist (or national communist; the second word no longer matters, since it is nothing but a historical relic; the expression "left-wing fascist" would serve as well, but it conveys even less meaning than the nationalist expressions) succeeded in doing for the Celestial Empire what Lenin had done for the Empire of the Tsars. The oldest bureaucratic apparatus in the world did not decompose into smaller units nor into colonies of other industrializers; it reemerged, greatly changed, as a People's Republic, as a beacon to "oppressed nations."

The Chairman and his Cadre followed the footsteps of a long line of predecessors and transformed the Celestial Empire into a vast source of preliminary capital, complete with purges, persecutions and their consequent great leaps forward.

The next stage, the launching of the capitalist production process, was carried out on the Russian model, namely by the national police. This did not work in China any better than it had in Russia. Apparently the entrepreneurial function has to be entrusted to confidence men or hustlers who are able to take other people in, and cops do not usually inspire the required confidence. But this was less important to Maoists than it had been to Leninists. The capitalist production process remains important, at least as important as the regularized drives for primitive accumulation, since without the capital there is no power, no nation. But the

Maoists make few, and ever fewer, claims for their model as a superior method of industrialization, and in this they are more modest than the Russians and less disappointed by the results of their industrial police.

The Maoist model offers itself to security guards and students the world over as a tried and tested methodology of power, as a scientific strategy of national liberation. Generally known as Mao-Zedong-Thought, [7] this science offers aspiring chairmen and cadres the prospect of unprecedented power over living beings, human activities and even thoughts. The pope and priests of the Catholic Church, with all their inquisitions and confessions, never had such power, not because they would have rejected it, but because they lacked the instruments made available by modern science and technology.

The liberation of the nation is the last stage in the elimination of parasites. Capitalism had already earlier cleared nature of parasites and reduced most of the rest of nature to raw materials for processing industries. Modern national socialism or social nationalism holds out the prospect of eliminating parasites from human society as well. The human parasites are usually sources of preliminary capital, but the capital is not always "material"; it can also be cultural or "spiritual." The ways, myths, poetry and music of the people are liquidated as a matter of course; some of the music and costumes of the former "folk culture" subsequently reappear, processed and packaged, as elements of the national spectacle, as decorations for the national accumulation drives; the ways and myths become raw materials for processing by one or several of the "human sciences." Even the useless resentment of workers toward their alienated wage labor is liquidated. When the nation is liberated, wage labor ceases to be an onerous burden and becomes a national obligation, to be carried out with joy. The inmates of a totally liberated nation read Orwell's 1984 as an anthropological study, a description of an earlier age.

It is no longer possible to satirize this state of affairs. Every satire risks becoming a bible for yet another national liberation front. [8] Every satirist risks becoming the founder of a new religion, a Buddha, Zarathustra, Jesus, Muhammad or Marx. Every exposure of the ravages of the dominant system, every critique of the system's functioning, becomes fodder for the horses of liberators, welding materials for builders of armies. Mao-Zedong-Thought in its numerous versions and revisions is a total science as well as a total theology; it is social physics as well as cosmic metaphysics. The French Committee of National Health claimed to embody the general will of only the French nation. The revisions of Mao-Zedong-Thought claim to embody the general will of all the world's oppressed.

The constant revisions of this Thought are necessary because its initial formulations were not applicable to all, or in fact to any, of the world's colonized populations. None of the world's colonized shared the Chinese heritage of having supported a state apparatus for the past two thousand years. Few of the world's oppressed had possessed any of the attributes of a nation in the recent or distant past. The Thought had to be adapted to people whose ancestors had lived without national chairmen, armies or police, without capitalist production processes and therefore without the need for preliminary capital.

These revisions were accomplished by enriching the initial Thought with borrowings from Mussolini, Hitler and the Zionist state of Israel. Mussolini's theory of the fulfillment of the nation in the state was a central tenet. All groups of people, whether small or large, industrial or non-industrial, concentrated or dispersed, were seen as nations, not in terms of their past, but in terms of their aura, their potentiality, a potentiality embedded in their national liberation fronts. Hitler's (and the Zionists') treatment of the nation as a racial entity was another central tenet. The cadres were recruited from among people depleted of their ancestors' kinships and customs, and consequently the liberators were not distinguishable from the oppressors in terms of language, beliefs, customs or weapons; the only welding material that held them to each other and to their mass base was the welding material that had held white servants to white bosses on the American frontier; the "racial bond" gave identities to those without identity, kinship to those who had no kin, community to those who had lost their community; it was the last bond of the culturally depleted.

The revised thought could now be applied to Africans as well as Navahos, Apaches as well as Palestinians. [9] The borrowings from Mussolini, Hitler and the Zionists are judiciously covered up, because Mussolini and Hitler failed to hold on to their seized power, and because the successful Zionists have turned their state into the world's policeman against all other national liberation fronts. Lenin, Stalin and Mao Zedong must be given even more credit than they deserve.

The revised and universally applicable models work much the same as the originals, but more smoothly; national liberation has become an applied science; the apparatus has been frequently tested; the numerous kinks in the originals have by now been straightened out. All that is needed to make the contraption run is a driver, a transmission belt, and fuel.

The driver is of course the theoretician himself, or his closest disciple. The transmission belt is the general staff, the organization, also called the Party or the communist party. This communist party with a small c is exactly what it is popularly understood to be. It is the nucleus of the police organization that does the purging and that will itself be purged once the leader becomes National Leader and needs to re-revise the invariant Thought while adapting himself to the family of nations, or at least to the family bankers, munitions suppliers and investors. And the fuel: the oppressed nation, the suffering masses, the liberated people are and will continue to be the fuel.

The leader and the general staff are not flown in from abroad; they are not foreign agitators. They are integral products of the capitalist production process. This production process has invariably been accompanied by racism. Racism is not a necessary component of production, but racism (in some form) has been a necessary component of the process of primitive accumulation of capital, and it has almost always leaked into the production process.

Industrialized nations have procured their preliminary capital by expropriating, deporting, persecuting and segregating, if not always by exterminating, people designated as legitimate prey. Kinships were broken, environments were destroyed, cultural orientations and ways were extirpated.

Descendants of survivors of such onslaughts are lucky if they preserve the merest relics, the most fleeting shadows of their ancestors' cultures. Many of the descendants do not retain even shadows; they are totally depleted; they go to work; they further enlarge the apparatus that destroyed their ancestors' culture. And in the world of work they are relegated to the margins, to the most unpleasant and least highly paid jobs. This makes them mad. A supermarket packer, for example, may know more about the stocks and the ordering than the manager, may know that racism is the only reason he is not manager and the manager not a packer. A security guard may know racism is the only reason he's not chief of police. It is among people who have lost all their roots, who dream themselves supermarket managers and chiefs of police, that the national liberation front takes root; this is where the leader and general staff are formed.

Nationalism continues to appeal to the depleted because other prospects appear bleaker. The culture of the ancestors was destroyed; therefore, by pragmatic standards, it failed; the only ancestors who survived were those who accommodated themselves to the invader's system, and they survived on the outskirts of garbage dumps. The varied utopias of poets and dreamers and the numerous "mythologies of the proletariat" have also failed; they have not proven themselves in practice; they have been nothing but hot air, pipe dreams, pies in the sky; the actual proletariat has been as racist as the bosses and the police.

The packer and the security guard have lost contact with the ancient culture; pipe dreams and utopias don't interest them, are in fact dismissed with the practical businessman's contempt toward poets, drifters and dreamers. Nationalism offers them something concrete, something that's been tried and tested and is known to work. There's no earthly reason for the descendants of the persecuted to remain persecuted when nationalism offers them the prospect of becoming persecutors. Near and distant relatives of victims can become a racist nation-state; they can themselves herd other people into concentration camps, push other people around at will, perpetrate genocidal war against them, procure preliminary capital by expropriating them. And if "racial relatives" of Hitler's victims can do it, so can the near and distant relatives of the victims of a Washington, Jackson, Reagan or Begin.

Every oppressed population can become a nation, a photographic negative of the oppressor nation, a place where the former packer is the supermarket's manager, where the former security guard is the chief of police. By applying the corrected strategy, every security guard can follow the precedent of ancient Rome's Praetorian guards. The security police of a foreign mining trust can proclaim itself a republic, liberate the people, and go on liberating them until they have nothing left but to pray for liberation to end. Even before the seizure of power, a gang can call itself a Front and offer heavily taxed and constantly policed poor people something they still lack: a tribute-gathering organization and a hit-squad, namely supplementary tax farmers and police, the people's own. In these ways, people can be liberated of the traits of their victimized ancestors; all the relics that still survive from pre-industrial times and non-capitalist cultures can at last be permanently extirpated.

The idea that an understanding of the genocide, that a memory of the holocausts, can only lead people to want to dismantle the system, is erroneous. The continuing appeal of nationalism suggests that the opposite is truer, namely that an understanding of genocide has led people to mobilize genocidal armies, that the memory of holocausts has led people to perpetrate holocausts. The sensitive poets who remembered the loss, the researchers who documented it, have been like the pure scientists who discovered the structure of the atom. Applied scientists used the discovery to split the atom's nucleus, to produce weapons which can split every atom's nucleus; nationalists used the poetry to split and fuse human populations, to mobilize genocidal armies, to perpetrate new holocausts.

The pure scientists, poets and researchers consider themselves innocent of the devastated countrysides and charred bodies.

Are they innocent?

It seems to me that at least one of Marx's observations is true: every minute devoted to the capitalist production process, every thought contributed to the industrial system, further enlarges a power that is inimical to nature, to culture, to life. Applied science is not something alien; it is an integral part of the capitalist production process. Nationalism is not flown in from abroad. It is a product of the capitalist production process, like the chemical agents poisoning the lakes, air, animals and people, like the nuclear plants radioactivating micro-environments in preparation for the radioactivation of the macro-environment.

As a postscript I'd like to answer a question before it is asked. The question is: "Don't you think a descendant of oppressed people is better off as a supermarket manager or police chief?" My answer is another question: What concentration camp manager, national executioner or torturer is not a descendant of oppressed people?

1984

[1] The subtitle of the first volume of *Capital* is *A Critique of Political Economy: The Process of Capitalist Production* (published by Charles H. Kerr & Co., 1906; republished by Random House, New York).

[2] in *Ibid.*, pages 784-850: Part VIII: "The So-Called Primitive Accumulation."

[3] E. Preobrazhensky, *The New Economics* (Moscow, 1926; English translation published by Clarendon Press, Oxford, 1965), a book which announced the fateful "law of primitive socialist accumulation."

[4] See V.I. Lenin, *The Development of Capitalism in Russia* (Moscow: Progress Publishers, 1964; first published in 1899). I quote from page 599: "If . . . we compare the present rapidity of development with that which could be achieved with the general level of technique and culture as it is today, the present rate of development of capitalism in Russia really must be considered as slow. And it cannot but be slow, for in no single capitalist country has there been such an abundant survival of ancient institutions that are incompatible with capitalism, retard its development, and immeasurably worsen the condition of the producers . . ."

[5] Or the liberation of the state: "Our myth is the nation, our myth is the greatness of the nation"; "It is the state which creates the nation, conferring volition and therefore real life on a people made aware of their moral unity"; "Always the maximum of liberty coincides with the maximum force of the state"; "Everything for the

state; nothing against the state; nothing outside the state." From *Che cosa è il fascismo* and *La dottrina del fascismo*, quoted by G. H. Sabine, *A History of Political Theory* (New York, 1955), pp. 872-878.

6 ". . . the gradual extension of our settlements will as certainly cause the savage, as the wolf, to retire; both being beasts of prey, tho' they differ in shape" (G. Washington in 1783). ". . . if ever we are constrained to lift the hatchet against any tribe, we will never lay it down till that tribe is exterminated, or driven beyond . . ." (T. Jefferson in 1807). ". . . the cruel massacres they have committed on the women and children of our frontiers taken by surprise, will oblige us now to pursue them to extermination, or drive them to new seats beyond our reach" (T. Jefferson in 1813). Quoted by Richard Drinnon in *Facing West: The Metaphysics of Indian-Hating and Empire Building* (New York: New American Library, 1980), pp. 65, 96, 98.

7 Readily available in paperback as *Quotations from Chairman Mao* (Peking: Political Department of the People's Liberation Army, 1966).

8 Black & Red tried to satirize this situation over ten years ago with the publication of a fake *Manual for Revolutionary Leaders*, a "how-to-do-it guide" whose author, Michael Velli, offered to do for the modern revolutionary prince what Machiavelli had offered the feudal prince. This phoney "Manual" fused Mao-Zedong-Thought with the Thought of Lenin, Stalin, Mussolini, Hitler and their modern followers, and offered grizzly recipes for the preparation of revolutionary organizations and the seizure of total power. Disconcertingly, at least half of the requests for this "Manual" came from aspiring national liberators, and it is possible that some of the current versions of the nationalist metaphysic contain recipes offered by Michael Velli.

9 I am not exaggerating. I have before me a book-length pamphlet titled *The Mythology of the White Proletariat: A Short Course for Understanding Babylon* by J. Sakai (Chicago: Morningstar Press, 1983). As an application of Mao-Zedong-Thought to American history, it is the most sensitive Maoist work I've seen. The author documents and describes, sometimes vividly, the oppression of America's enslaved Africans, the deportations and exterminations of the American continent's indigenous inhabitants, the racist exploitation of Chinese, the incarceration of Japanese-Americans in concentration camps. The author mobilizes all these experiences of unmitigated terror, not to look for ways to supersede the system that perpetrated them, but to urge the victims to reproduce the same system among themselves. Sprinkled with pictures and quotations of chairmen Lenin, Stalin, Mao Zedong and Ho-chi Minh, this work makes no attempt to hide or disguise its repressive aims; it urges Africans as well as Navahos, Apaches as well as Palestinians, to organize a party, seize state power, and liquidate parasites.